Descubra Juegos Gratis Online

Disponibles Aquí:

BestActivityBooks.com/FREEGAMES

5 CONSEJOS PARA EMPEZAR

1) CÓMO RESOLVER LAS SOPA DE LETRAS

Los rompecabezas tienen un formato clásico:

- Las palabras se ocultan sin espacios ni guiones,...
- Orientación: Las palabras pueden escribirse hacia delante, hacia atrás, hacia arriba, hacia abajo o en diagonal (pueden estar invertidas).
- Las palabras pueden superponerse o cruzarse.

2) APRENDIZAJE ACTIVO

Junto a cada palabra hay un espacio para anotar la traducción. Para fomentar un aprendizaje activo, un **DICCIONARIO** al final de esta edición te permitirá comprobar y ampliar tus conocimientos. Busca y anota las traducciones, encuéntralas en el puzzle y añádelas a tu vocabulario!

3) MARCAR LAS PALABRAS

Puedes inventar tu propio sistema de marcado. ¿Quizás ya usas uno? También puedes, por ejemplo, marcar las palabras difíciles de encontrar con una cruz, las que te gustan con una estrella, las nuevas con un triángulo, las raras con un diamante, etc.

4) ESTRUCTURAR EL APRENDIZAJE

Esta edición ofrece un **CUADERNO DE NOTAS** muy práctico al final del libro. En vacaciones, de viaje o en casa, podrás organizar fácilmente tus nuevos conocimientos sin necesidad de un segundo cuaderno!

5) ¿HABÉIS TERMINADO TODAS LAS PARRILLAS?

En las últimas páginas de este libro, en la sección **DESAFÍO FINAL**, encontrarás un juego gratis!

¡Rápido y sencillo! Echa un vistazo a nuestra colección de libros de actividades para tu próximo momento de diversión y aprendizaje, ¡a sólo un clic de distancia!

Encuentre su próximo reto en:

BestActivityBooks.com/MiProximoLibro

En sus marcas, listos, ¡Ya!

¿Sabías que hay unas 7.000 lenguas diferentes en el mundo? Las palabras son preciosas.

Nos encantan los idiomas y hemos trabajado duro para crear libros de la más alta calidad para tí. ¿Nuestros ingredientes?

Una selección de temas adecuados para el aprendizaje, tres buenas porciones de entretenimiento, y luego añadimos una cucharada de palabras difíciles y una pizca de palabras raras. Los servimos con cariño y máxima diversión para que puedas resolver los mejores juegos de palabras y te diviertas aprendiendo!

Tu opinión es esencial. Puedes participar activamente en el éxito de este libro dejándonos un comentario. Nos encantaría saber qué es lo que más le ha gustado de esta edición.

Aquí hay un enlace rápido a tu página de pedidos:

BestBooksActivity.com/Opiniones50

Gracias por tu ayuda y diviértete!

Todo el equipo

1 - Arqueología

```
O W N U O K E N T P M A O C
C B M O T F L O E U Y N R I
O K J N C D R I M M S T E V
U B B E A R E T P B T I S I
A D B T C N U A L J E Q E L
W E O T U A U E R R U A I
K S N O N R S L Z O Y I R Z
T C E G K E R A Y S Z T C A
E E S R N P A V R S O Y H T
A N Z O O X E E N E I X E I
M D V F W E Y R P F L S R O
V A O O N N M A P O M I I N
Y N F O S S I L T R U J C C
C T S M U C V Y J P O X P V
```

ANALYSIS
ANTIQUITY
YEARS
CIVILIZATION
DESCENDANT
UNKNOWN
TEAM
ERA
EVALUATION
EXPERT

FOSSIL
BONES
RESEARCHER
MYSTERY
OBJECTS
FORGOTTEN
PROFESSOR
RELIC
TEMPLE
TOMB

2 - Granja #2

```
S O F H G C O J S I T Z T A
H M R R S E Y E L R A B R U
E E E C U P L C T R L A A P
E A M S H I I T W I M N C J
P D R F W A T Q N G P I T W
S O A O V D R K M A A M O H
H W F O X V C D M T B A R E
E C K D L L A M A I E L W A
P R C O R N R A B O E S W T
H N A M O C I P I N H G Q F
E W M G I Q Q S C E I H V I
R L A M B L T W Y U V R P J
D F R I Y R K C U D E N K X
U P V E G E T A B L E D W K
```

FARMER	LLAMA
ANIMALS	CORN
BARLEY	SHEEP
BEEHIVE	SHEPHERD
FOOD	DUCK
LAMB	MEADOW
FRUIT	IRRIGATION
BARN	TRACTOR
ORCHARD	WHEAT
MILK	VEGETABLE

3 - La Empresa

```
V  B  R  I  S  K  S  B  H  E  L  V  G  E
P  R  O  F  E  S  S  I  O  N  A  L  L  F
N  T  I  N  N  O  V  A  T  I  V  E  O  T
D  C  P  R  O  G  R  E  S  S  L  A  B  D
E  U  N  E  V  E  R  I  W  T  P  G  A  H
V  D  U  O  Q  U  A  L  I  T  Y  B  L  F
I  O  M  T  I  I  N  D  U  S  T  R  Y  N
T  R  E  N  D  S  E  C  R  U  O  S  E  R
A  P  V  I  N  O  I  T  A  T  U  P  E  R
E  U  N  I  T  S  F  C  N  D  X  H  D  G
R  N  T  N  E  M  T  S  E  V  N  I  P  P
C  B  U  S  I  N  E  S  S  D  R  Z  X  D
E  M  P  L  O  Y  M  E  N  T  O  N  J  T
P  O  S  S  I  B  I  L  I  T  Y  Z  T  B
```

QUALITY	POSSIBILITY
CREATIVE	PRODUCT
DECISION	PROFESSIONAL
EMPLOYMENT	PROGRESS
GLOBAL	RESOURCES
INDUSTRY	REPUTATION
REVENUE	RISKS
INNOVATIVE	TRENDS
INVESTMENT	UNITS
BUSINESS	

4 - Mueble

```
F A D H W J Z J I J Y W E C
B U R I A H C H A M M O C K
O E T M F M C B C C X L D S
O J N O O T G R U O V L C E
B E D C N I V S R U W I O D
L D V I H R R S T C I P M S
D R E S S E R E A H N N F I
A R M C H A I R I S K M O U
M I R R O R L T N A X E R Y
S H E L V E S T S K A B T H
Q J W V A F B A D B S R E R
L A M P M G S M C Z A U R U
C U S H I O N S S R E W S G
B O O K C A S E O E S P T Z
```

RUG	DESK
PILLOW	MIRROR
ARMOIRE	BOOKCASE
BENCH	SHELVES
BED	FUTON
CUSHIONS	HAMMOCK
MATTRESS	LAMP
CURTAINS	CHAIR
DRESSER	ARMCHAIR
COMFORTERS	COUCH

5 - Aviones

```
P C F E C D P I L O T J R A
A Y Z N R H I N X T T Q E L
S H Q G F Y S R G A N X R T
S I F I Q Z C A E W J H E I
E S G N I D N A L C G I H T
N T A E C R E W I B T T P U
G O U M D Z C Z R R G I S D
E R H J O T U C X A S H O E
R Y H Y D R O G E N K E M N
B A L L O O N C F N Y I T G
A D V E N T U R E N D G A I
J T E W U K E R J Z T H T S
B M E O F F L S R K E T J E
C O N S T R U C T I O N Z D
```

AIR
ALTITUDE
HEIGHT
LANDING
ATMOSPHERE
ADVENTURE
SKY
FUEL
CONSTRUCTION

DIRECTION
DESIGN
BALLOON
HYDROGEN
HISTORY
ENGINE
PASSENGER
PILOT
CREW

6 - Tipos de Cabello

```
C B U K N T J D M G R L D B
D U R C B I T L Y N I H S R
R K R A W L Z O H O S S I A
Y G Z L I B M U T L K O L I
N O A B S D N O L B S Z V D
C U R L Y J E Y A R G M E S
P Z T C A Y E D E Y Q E R A
P L E B H V E R H J D Y H W
T F B D L A B C Y M C T D W
C T H H Q W A K D O I R W M
Q O Z Y T Z H C V N W O R B
E Q S S G H F I P M R H F M
W P K O L N I H T F O S A S
K W A Y W Y M T I E J I U V
```

WHITE	WAVY
SHINY	SILVER
BALD	CURLY
SHORT	CURLS
THIN	BLOND
GRAY	HEALTHY
THICK	DRY
LONG	SOFT
BROWN	BRAIDED
BLACK	BRAIDS

7 - Ética

```
R O P T I M I S M B O M C D
X R E C N E I T A P V M O I
S E A H O V A L U E S J M G
I A T L I R E A L I S M P N
N S O Y T S E N O H Z A A I
T O L T A R W I S D O M S T
E N E I R O U R T D C M S Y
G A R N E R B I T A W J I P
R B A A P P T V S P S N O I
I L N M O S T Z G M A C N U
T E C U O K I N D N E S S B
Y S E H C I T A M O L P I D
I N D I V I D U A L I S M B
R A T I O N A L I T Y M E T
```

ALTRUISM	INTEGRITY
KINDNESS	OPTIMISM
COMPASSION	PATIENCE
COOPERATION	RATIONALITY
DIGNITY	REASONABLE
DIPLOMATIC	REALISM
HONESTY	WISDOM
HUMANITY	TOLERANCE
INDIVIDUALISM	VALUES

8 - Ciencia Ficción

```
W K T D D R F B T P I R D M
K B Y U O V A O F L L E C Y
E Q G V Y F N O U A L A A S
S T O B O R T K T N U L H T
F Q L H P T A S U E S I A E
J A O F E N S N R T I S T R
C I N E M A T U I P O T O I
G P H R E T I J S G N I M O
A O C I R S C U T G A C I U
L T E F T I Y S I V A M C S
A U T O X D C A C M K Z I R
X M M J E O R A C L E S D G
Y E X P L O S I O N S A N R
L W O R L D O S J P V V Z C
```

ATOMIC
CINEMA
DISTANT
EXPLOSION
EXTREME
FANTASTIC
FIRE
FUTURISTIC
GALAXY
ILLUSION

IMAGINARY
BOOKS
MYSTERIOUS
WORLD
ORACLE
PLANET
REALISTIC
ROBOTS
TECHNOLOGY
UTOPIA

9 - Circo

```
A K W X R T C S T G N Y B C
V C C R R I E V N C G T B O
G F R B X G O I A B Z E B S
M G P O L E Z S H O W N A T
C A T Y B R I W P V Z T L U
P A G N I A T R E T N E L M
A A N I O E T Y L X D Z O E
R N O D C F T N E D R E O R
A I I Q Y I M O N K E Y N T
D M L D Q T A O B C L S S R
E A C L O W N N Y Q G R L I
A L U E M U S I C I G A M C
I S L H Q C L F R N U F Z K
S P E C T A T O R R J I U U
```

ACROBAT
ANIMALS
CANDY
TENT
PARADE
ELEPHANT
ENTERTAIN
SPECTATOR
BALLOONS
LION

MAGIC
MAGICIAN
JUGGLER
MONKEY
SHOW
MUSIC
CLOWN
TIGER
COSTUME
TRICK

10 - Granja #1

```
O I Q Z X P W L F F E G Z C
D W Z U A K P V E T R L K H
S O H O J V E K R J U T L I
N R N L A N D C T O T A C C
H C Q K B W C O I M L O C K
S X P U E A C W L R U G A E
W A T E R Y A H I F C E L N
H O N E Y B F S Z I I R F E
G Q S H O R S E E B R E R E
W L E Z I B F P R E G G L Q
M V A H J F E U L E A O D D
D O G X L A N F J I Y B W S
Z C G U R J C Q X T T Y B G
S E E D S L E Y Y F N C L C
```

BEE   CAT
AGRICULTURE   HAY
WATER   HONEY
RICE   DOG
DONKEY   CHICKEN
HORSE   SEEDS
GOAT   CALF
FIELD   LAND
CROW   COW
FERTILIZER   FENCE

11 - Camping

```
R R O M V G J A F P Z C G E
N O O M H I H G N I T N U H
A A P I O U P U F I Q V H U
D G T E O N A C I H M D F A
V R N U H W B O R A M A N G
E S E E R T K F E M A H L T
N S M H Z E K A L M P A C S
T A P N U M V G U O I T A E
U P I L U A C B X C L K L R
R M U F I W I F X K B L T O
E O Q Q S D L N L Q K L R F
T C E S N I R E T D Y F P C
L A N T E R N I A T N U O M
H P C A B I N A X R O E J X
```

ANIMALS
ADVENTURE
TREES
FOREST
COMPASS
CABIN
CANOE
HUNTING
ROPE
EQUIPMENT

FIRE
HAMMOCK
INSECT
LAKE
LANTERN
MOON
MAP
MOUNTAIN
NATURE
HAT

12 - Fruta

```
N A V Y G N F Z C M Z M E C
S R V T D Y C B O W E G L Y
P A N O J X T N C V P L G N
X S H C C L V N O X A P O N
S P B I F A D N N B R M V N
E B K R D B D E U P G A G O
L E F P C V U O T Y J N F M
P R W A I H A G U A V A A E
P R K N O E E S Q M B N W L
A Y P V G M L R A E P A M F
E O R A N G E Y R R E B O T
N E C T A R I N E Y K I W I
I L W Q M U A P P L E X N U
P E A C H P A P A Y A A A P
```

AVOCADO	APPLE
APRICOT	PEACH
BERRY	MELON
CHERRY	ORANGE
COCONUT	NECTARINE
RASPBERRY	PAPAYA
GUAVA	PEAR
KIWI	PINEAPPLE
LEMON	BANANA
MANGO	GRAPE

13 - Geología

```
C B S T A L A C T I T E O K
R N O C Z V S L A R E N I M
Y L P E C V A O I S F O S C
S Z V L R C V L X U Z T S B
T L R Q E O L W E R X S H G
A A A O S R S D Q U A R T Z
L Y O C Y W E I S R N Z F P
S E N R E V A C O K W C O C
J R G H G N Y A S N M M S O
C O N T I N E N T A X W S R
R W N C K U A E T A L P I A
S T A L A G M I T E S T L L
C A L C I U M V O L C A N O
E A R T H Q U A K E D A P G
```

ACID
CALCIUM
LAYER
CAVERN
CONTINENT
CORAL
CRYSTALS
QUARTZ
EROSION
STALACTITE

STALAGMITES
FOSSIL
GEYSER
LAVA
PLATEAU
MINERALS
STONE
SALT
EARTHQUAKE
VOLCANO

14 - Álgebra

```
M F P P P I M A R G A I D I
Z Z I R B Q R A E N I L L N
G C A O I N O I T A U Q E F
O N X B Z E R O F R O R K I
I D D L L E S L A F I P C N
W B G E R H C J C M M X Y I
U O S M U N O I T U L O S T
N U M B E R D A O L C J F E
F R A C T I O N R H M R O D
D I V I S I O N E V I R R F
S U B T R A C T I O N K M E
Z P A R E N T H E S I S U S
M V E E X P O N E N T E L D
S I M P L I F Y H M C S A Y
```

ZERO
DIAGRAM
DIVISION
EQUATION
EXPONENT
FACTOR
FALSE
FORMULA
FRACTION

INFINITE
LINEAR
MATRIX
NUMBER
PARENTHESIS
PROBLEM
SUBTRACTION
SIMPLIFY
SOLUTION

15 - Plantas

```
V F K A T G F L O W E R C Q
E E Y W L D R U O O B M A B
G R Z L E G B A R O L F C X
E T M K A H D E S V Q W T G
T I N Y F T O O R S X N U T
A L I Z T H S E R O F S R
T I Z I G A R D E N Y Z G E
I Z T R J O D I S B B V M E
O E H Y H P E T A L A R I R
N R I M C B E B L J Y U D N
G M O S S B O T A N Y Q W F
B U S H F O L I A G E Y A I
N K P A G M D T Q D O V I W
B E A N C X T Z F Y B F A D
```

BUSH	FOLIAGE
TREE	BEAN
BAMBOO	IVY
BERRY	GRASS
FOREST	LEAF
BOTANY	GARDEN
CACTUS	MOSS
FERTILIZER	PETAL
FLOWER	ROOT
FLORA	VEGETATION

16 - Suministros de Arte

```
C K F G U C K W A Z Y F U B
R E T A W O N I R S W S Z Z
E T V W O L I O E U L G L M
A K A N R O F C M C V A E A
T O C B G R E P A P H X I C
I P E Y L S G A C H A I R R
V U P A W E I D E A S Y B Y
I B A L S T N I A P G N P L
T R S C M E A E G W Q S U I
Y U T H J S L K E P D F V C
F S E W A T E R C O L O R S
E H L P E N C I L S J H R F
V E S E R A S E R T B U S G
O S C Z P O D I D G B I Z D
```

OIL	CREATIVITY
ACRYLIC	IDEAS
WATERCOLORS	PENCILS
WATER	TABLE
CLAY	PAPER
ERASER	PASTELS
EASEL	GLUE
CAMERA	PAINTS
BRUSHES	CHAIR
COLORS	INK

17 - Negocio

```
F  K  T  A  X  E  S  F  C  C  M  X  B  R
C  A  I  S  W  G  E  I  U  M  E  O  U  B
A  L  C  J  A  M  Y  N  R  D  R  E  D  P
R  L  J  T  B  L  T  A  R  H  C  U  G  Q
E  S  D  S  O  Y  E  N  E  B  H  H  E  E
E  A  K  O  J  R  R  C  N  D  A  C  T  M
R  G  Q  C  U  Y  Y  E  C  O  N  O  N  P
I  N  P  O  B  N  U  P  Y  F  D  M  U  L
E  C  O  N  O  M  I  C  S  F  I  P  O  O
D  D  H  P  F  F  L  D  Q  I  S  A  C  Y
I  I  S  N  P  K  P  U  G  C  E  N  S  E
K  L  R  E  Y  O  L  P  M  E  S  Y  I  E
T  R  A  N  S  A  C  T  I  O  N  M  D  F
R  V  Y  D  M  O  N  E  Y  M  I  U  O  I
```

CAREER	TAXES
COST	MERCHANDISE
DISCOUNT	CURRENCY
MONEY	OFFICE
ECONOMICS	BUDGET
EMPLOYEE	SHOP
EMPLOYER	JOB
COMPANY	TRANSACTION
FACTORY	SALE
FINANCE	

18 - Jardín

```
T I D K W Q N G I N H Y E W
E R R C S X E E R C S O I L
R X A O I I R R E A R I T A
R J H M Y Z V Z K J S B N A
H T C M P G A R A G E S N K
O E R A G O G A R D E N Y W
S R O H G S L F C S N U Y E
E R E B T H M I L B U S H E
A A V G U O T D N O P O H D
V C B I L V U J W E W O B S
O E S L M E T E A C F E D E
P O R C H L R H L N D U R H
M L W J Z P E U B E N C H Z
J K B U T I E H C F T R V C
```

BUSH
TREE
BENCH
LAWN
POND
FLOWER
GARAGE
HAMMOCK
GRASS
ORCHARD

GARDEN
WEEDS
HOSE
SHOVEL
PORCH
RAKE
SOIL
TERRACE
TRAMPOLINE
FENCE

19 - Países #2

```
U P A K I S T A N F N X S L
R K A E O A L B A N I A T V
B R R A U S T R A L I A A D
Z D N A L E R I T A L L F T
M A E I I L L A G U T R O P
U I X S O N A D U S P P C A
D S A S C Y E N C T D R I C
J E D U J E C E E R G N X Q
A N N R T T N M H I H O E L
M O A M D M A A J A H B M A
A D G H A O R L P C O Y B O
I N U N U R F Z K A I R Y S
C I Y R R C K V W L J M V T
A I P O I H T E W N Y J J S
```

ALBANIA
AUSTRALIA
AUSTRIA
DENMARK
ETHIOPIA
FRANCE
GREECE
INDONESIA
IRELAND
JAMAICA

JAPAN
LAOS
MEXICO
PAKISTAN
PORTUGAL
RUSSIA
SYRIA
SUDAN
UKRAINE
UGANDA

20 - Números

```
P O T W E N T Y X T F Y V S
I R U O F D K V K W Z I T R
N E E T N E V E S E R I V X
S Z P H E S N M I L N Q C E
I Z Y G E L E I X V N I N E
X C Q I T H E V Q E T A L F
T W W E E L T V E S F E N I
E K S O N Q R I W N F G N Y
E T W O I N U L A M I C E D
N J K A N T O O L D F R R G
E T Q N D E F B N I T V N S
W O C N E E T H G I E G J U
X T H R E E O T F N E T Q M
T H I R T E E N T K N V N V
```

FOURTEEN   TWELVE
ZERO   TWO
FIVE   NINE
FOUR   EIGHT
DECIMAL   FIFTEEN
NINETEEN   SIX
EIGHTEEN   SEVEN
SIXTEEN   THIRTEEN
SEVENTEEN   THREE
TEN   TWENTY

21 - Física

```
B Y C H E M I C A L G X V T
Y G T A G O K H O M A B W M
C T D Z K T G E G E S F P A
N E I E L A S R E V I N U G
E N E V M E C H A N I C S N
U G C H A O S S A M A K T E
Q I D N L R L H M J N W P T
E N E X U A G L F I T W Q I
R E N W M E L C I T R A P S
F Z S K R L N T S N H E C M
Z R I V O C Q P C N Q D E E
J G T M F U V E L O C I T Y
V A Y E L N O R T C E L E E
F W M O L E C U L E I I U H
```

ATOM
CHAOS
DENSITY
ELECTRON
FORMULA
FREQUENCY
GAS
GRAVITY
MAGNETISM

MASS
MECHANICS
MOLECULE
ENGINE
NUCLEAR
PARTICLE
CHEMICAL
UNIVERSAL
VELOCITY

22 - Belleza

```
U F E C N A R G A R F I U K
B F P U S K I N J G E B N J
P Y X R O L O C T R K Z L F
B H E L C V X X J A O I L S
S X O S J H B P H C C Q C E
N T X T S Y T O O E P N O L
L T Y M O E O O P M A H S E
U G K L K G R U A R F C M G
R O R R I M E V K A F N E A
S C E N T S G N I H C U T N
B I P I W G T V I C F X I T
M A K E U P E F J C E P C I
M A S C A R A M G M Q S S K
J V L I P S T I C K N O M J
```

OILS
SCENT
SHAMPOO
COLOR
COSMETICS
ELEGANT
CHARM
MIRROR
STYLIST

PHOTOGENIC
FRAGRANCE
GRACE
MAKEUP
SKIN
LIPSTICK
CURLS
MASCARA
SERVICES

23 - Países #1

```
B  B  S  G  D  Y  G  D  I  D  U  L  A  B
U  M  S  I  A  P  A  N  A  M  A  I  R  R
M  O  R  O  C  C  O  A  I  U  Z  B  G  A
H  E  C  O  S  Q  P  L  D  I  Y  Y  E  Z
O  I  G  A  D  K  A  O  N  G  N  A  N  I
N  S  A  Y  N  A  B  P  I  L  A  M  T  L
D  K  L  A  P  A  U  Q  C  E  M  E  I  M
U  P  E  W  C  T  D  C  Z  B  R  C  N  G
R  H  U  R  Y  F  P  A  E  Z  E  R  A  A
A  D  Z  O  N  I  C  A  R  A  G  U  A  C
S  S  E  N  I  P  P  I  L  I  H  P  D  U
U  F  N  G  A  I  T  A  L  Y  X  A  W  K
V  G  E  J  P  B  Q  R  R  F  I  N  M  E
M  W  V  L  S  H  Y  M  I  D  Z  X  B  F
```

GERMANY	INDIA
ARGENTINA	ITALY
BELGIUM	LIBYA
BRAZIL	MALI
CANADA	MOROCCO
ECUADOR	NICARAGUA
EGYPT	NORWAY
SPAIN	PANAMA
PHILIPPINES	POLAND
HONDURAS	VENEZUELA

24 - Mitología

```
G N U Y T I L A T R O M M I
C R E A T I O N T Y Q O C M
R E V E N G E T S S B R R O
L K D I R R E D N U H T E N
U U O R H E R O M O T A A S
E H G C O O D R F L G L T T
L A B Y R I N T H A N C U E
U Q L P I Z V R O E E U R R
H E A V E N K A X J R L E C
D I S A S T E R H P T T L T
L I G H T N I N G E S U M P
A R C H E T Y P E U B R M L
B E L I E F S R O A L E X R
L E G E N D W A R R I O R M
```

ARCHETYPE	WARRIOR
JEALOUSY	HERO
HEAVEN	IMMORTALITY
BEHAVIOR	LABYRINTH
CREATION	LEGEND
BELIEFS	MONSTER
CREATURE	MORTAL
CULTURE	LIGHTNING
DISASTER	THUNDER
STRENGTH	REVENGE

25 - Ecología

```
P  J  M  S  A  M  S  E  I  C  E  P  S  G
N  L  P  H  C  L  I  M  A  T  E  A  U  L
D  E  A  E  A  V  A  R  I  E  T  Y  R  O
E  R  G  N  U  B  Y  M  E  M  C  R  V  B
X  U  O  L  T  C  I  Y  L  N  O  E  I  A
B  T  F  U  N  S  J  T  B  O  M  S  V  L
P  A  Z  J  G  J  Z  I  A  I  M  O  A  I
Z  N  W  Q  L  H  H  S  N  T  U  U  L  M
M  A  R  I  N  E  T  R  I  A  N  R  J  K
N  A  T  U  R  A  L  E  A  T  I  C  K  U
M  A  R  S  H  N  F  V  T  E  T  E  L  K
Q  F  M  M  U  U  D  I  S  G  I  S  X  B
B  F  L  O  R  A  V  D  U  E  E  G  U  T
X  J  J  T  A  F  M  G  S  V  S  K  R  I
```

CLIMATE
COMMUNITIES
DIVERSITY
SPECIES
FAUNA
FLORA
GLOBAL
HABITAT
MARINE
NATURAL

NATURE
MARSH
PLANTS
RESOURCES
DROUGHT
SUSTAINABLE
SURVIVAL
VARIETY
VEGETATION

26 - Casa

```
K N B B R M K I F H G M N G
R N A W I I E B R E L E B A
O P S I Y R O O L F N Z Q R
O D E N L R B R O O M C U D
F O M D M O O R D E B I E E
Z O E O J R F E G P I T K N
F R N W A L C W S A Q T S C
V A T W Y P K O A W R A O B
H N U M D V Q H U V F A G O
T B Y C Y O T S B Y R J G H
R U G S E C A L P E R I F E
U O L T B T H L M G W G V F
L I B R A R Y A A I S E X V
K I T C H E N W L O G X G K
```

RUG
ATTIC
LIBRARY
FIREPLACE
KITCHEN
BEDROOM
SHOWER
BROOM
MIRROR
GARAGE

FAUCET
GARDEN
LAMP
WALL
FLOOR
DOOR
BASEMENT
ROOF
FENCE
WINDOW

27 - Salud y Bienestar #2

```
P V H D R N I M A T I V S D
E S M O N X U X S I H B T I
M S V O S Y H T L A E H R S
X A R L G P T Y R Q Q E E E
E P S B U G I P T I T N S A
N P C G G V G T G X T Y S S
E E I R O L A C A E E I G E
R T T W K D Z Y W L I D O I
G I E G A S S A M E D A F N
Y T N A L L E R G Y I Z L K
G E E R E C O V E R Y G H J
I V G D I G E S T I O N H U
E I H I N F E C T I O N J T
H Y G I E N E A N A T O M Y
```

ALLERGY
ANATOMY
APPETITE
CALORIE
DIET
DIGESTION
ENERGY
DISEASE
STRESS
GENETICS

HYGIENE
HOSPITAL
INFECTION
MASSAGE
NUTRITION
WEIGHT
RECOVERY
HEALTHY
BLOOD
VITAMIN

28 - Selva Tropical

```
W Y U S S O M S L A M M A M
C O M M U N I T Y M T E O S
N A G T X O M O S P L G Z G
A C S F W I N Y L H G U M H
T E Q J T T J E T I R F C W
U T V U J A N E G B G E G I
R A W W V V L A V I V R U S
E M F S H R C S D A D E Z J
B I R D S E H I U N U N N U
Z L I U G S C S V S X J I N
N C T O S E S P E C I E S G
X X J L A R I N S E C T S L
B F C C D P R E S P E C T E
D I V E R S I T Y M G H W A
```

AMPHIBIANS
CLIMATE
COMMUNITY
DIVERSITY
SPECIES
INDIGENOUS
INSECTS
MAMMALS
MOSS

NATURE
CLOUDS
BIRDS
PRESERVATION
REFUGE
RESPECT
JUNGLE
SURVIVAL

29 - Colores

```
Z Y C A P Z F U G G N B M D
O G G E D L O Z C X W L A N
B R O W N O S M I R C U G A
G F A X P U R P L E Y E E A
V R C Y A N K S P E Y J N Z
K I E G N A R O B N E X T U
S E O E A S O G E E L P A R
O E T L N W V I I B L U G E
L Z P H E E A D G L O C R X
K X F I A T W N E A W Z E I
L O C W A P B I O C E G Y P
F U C H S I A L W K N I P H
R E D I Q V B B W H I T E E
I B N M I M H K J Q H A O T
```

YELLOW	MAGENTA
BLUE	BROWN
AZURE	ORANGE
BEIGE	BLACK
WHITE	PURPLE
CRIMSON	RED
CYAN	PINK
FUCHSIA	SEPIA
GREY	GREEN
INDIGO	VIOLET

30 - Adjetivos #1

```
Y  G  U  B  B  A  A  B  S  O  L  U  T  E
O  E  J  K  O  R  M  Z  B  D  N  C  M  V
U  N  F  X  B  H  I  B  F  N  E  I  S  I
N  E  E  P  U  U  L  G  I  W  H  T  L  T
G  R  P  Y  F  G  A  Q  H  T  C  A  O  C
F  O  C  D  E  E  R  H  C  T  I  M  W  A
V  U  D  A  R  K  G  O  M  V  J  O  R  G
H  S  W  Y  A  A  E  M  U  P  P  R  U  L
E  O  E  V  I  T  C  A  R  T  T  A  P  S
S  E  N  A  P  E  R  F  E  C  T  M  Q  Q
S  B  F  E  C  I  N  N  O  C  E  N  T  N
W  B  Z  H  S  U  O  I  R  E  S  A  K  H
N  W  E  O  H  T  N  A  T  R  O  P  M  I
E  J  R  M  O  D  E  R  N  Z  U  H  E  P
```

ABSOLUTE
ACTIVE
AMBITIOUS
AROMATIC
ATTRACTIVE
BRIGHT
HUGE
GENEROUS
LARGE
HONEST

IMPORTANT
INNOCENT
YOUNG
SLOW
MODERN
DARK
PERFECT
HEAVY
SERIOUS

31 - Familia

```
N E P H E W A H U S B A N D
F A T H E R W N U N C L E S
C C G N D E U W C J U I Q I
O H R C A H Q F A E I N N S
U I A C U T S H J I S K K T
S L N H G O P E F I W T V E
I D D I H M M C U N K U O R
N H F L T D A E S O J G R R
C O A D E N T I P S U J E W
D O T R R A E N N D L I H C
O D H E E R R K U N W B T L
J Q E N I G N L F A R D O K
D A R E L Z A C F R A N R O
M O T H E R L G C G K A B S
```

GRANDMOTHER
GRANDFATHER
ANCESTOR
WIFE
SISTER
BROTHER
DAUGHTER
CHILDHOOD
MOTHER
HUSBAND

MATERNAL
GRANDSON
CHILD
CHILDREN
FATHER
COUSIN
NIECE
NEPHEW
AUNT
UNCLE

32 - Disciplinas Científicas

```
A R C H A E O L O G Y U G Y
P H Y S I O L O G Y C M B X
K A H A V Y R T S I M E H C
N U T R I T I O N S W C T Y
I M M U N O L O G Y H H P G
M P S Y C H O L O G Y A H O
K N P S C I T S I U G N I L
S O C I O L O G Y A J I I O
G E O L O G Y G O L O C E I
A S T R O N O M Y D T S X B
N C D M E T E O R O L O G Y
N E U R O L O G Y N A T O B
B I O C H E M I S T R Y N D
M I N E R A L O G Y L S Y J
```

ARCHAEOLOGY	LINGUISTICS
ASTRONOMY	MECHANICS
BIOLOGY	METEOROLOGY
BIOCHEMISTRY	MINERALOGY
BOTANY	NEUROLOGY
ECOLOGY	NUTRITION
PHYSIOLOGY	PSYCHOLOGY
GEOLOGY	CHEMISTRY
IMMUNOLOGY	SOCIOLOGY

33 - Cocina

```
S P O O N S W B A G B B J R
K J C U P S T S Q I A T Y E
R U F O O D O O A A P N D F
O G A O E R E Z E E R F Z R
F C C N E X A R L Q O V W I
D X N Q K S T L D G N F R G
J D S S Q X P W A P S S O E
G R E B B O W O L N P M Z E
N X C Y P R E B N G R E M A
A A I G H J L I M G R P G T
V M P E N F T A D M E I B O
F K S K C I T S P O H C L R
X H G V I X E V J C U E X L
I S E V I N K O V E N R P L
```

KETTLE	OVEN
TO EAT	JUG
FOOD	CHOPSTICKS
FREEZER	GRILL
SPOONS	RECIPE
LADLE	REFRIGERATOR
KNIVES	NAPKIN
APRON	CUPS
SPICES	BOWL
SPONGE	FORKS

34 - Moda

```
S O P H I S T I C A T E D M
M E A S U R E M E N T S G O
L C L Q E B O U T I Q U E D
A W O V G M P E X F P J L E
C P Z U Q L B A L U G N P R
E M O D E S T R T E A L M N
O R I G I N A L O T G H I P
V L S F A B R I C I E A S H
M I N I M A L I S T D R N Y
S F O T E X T U R E N E N T
F X T Q W U O C B H E R R V
K T T L A C I T C A R P W Y
G D U A V N G N I H T O L C
A Y B S T Y L E W H Z Z O Y
```

EMBROIDERY
BUTTONS
BOUTIQUE
ELEGANT
LACE
STYLE
MEASUREMENTS
MINIMALIST
MODERN
MODEST

ORIGINAL
PATTERN
PRACTICAL
CLOTHING
SIMPLE
SOPHISTICATED
FABRIC
TREND
TEXTURE

35 - Electricidad

```
Q  J  P  L  Z  G  D  S  A  P  E  D  V  V
M  U  M  H  I  I  K  W  O  T  S  O  H  E
M  I  A  Z  V  E  O  P  J  C  W  F  D  V
A  Y  L  N  Y  W  P  X  H  C  K  K  P  I
G  G  A  A  T  F  V  A  E  M  Z  E  A  T
N  N  O  I  S  I  V  E  L  E  T  P  T  I
E  P  W  C  T  V  T  O  B  J  E  C  T  S
T  N  I  I  O  O  E  Y  A  U  Y  F  K  O
C  E  R  R  R  E  L  E  C  T  R  I  C  P
Y  T  E  T  A  G  E  N  E  R  A  T  O  R
G  W  S  C  G  B  A  T  T  E  R  Y  L  P
I  O  Z  E  E  E  Q  U  I  P  M  E  N  T
A  R  B  L  U  B  N  E  G  A  T  I  V  E
S  K  R  E  S  A  L  O  Q  M  D  P  P  Q
```

STORAGE	GENERATOR
BATTERY	MAGNET
BULB	LAMP
CABLE	LASER
WIRES	NEGATIVE
QUANTITY	OBJECTS
ELECTRICIAN	POSITIVE
ELECTRIC	NETWORK
SOCKET	TELEVISION
EQUIPMENT	

36 - Salud y Bienestar #1

```
H A B I T M I O B E R V R T
Y A E Q E R U T S O P I E R
Q U C J R N D S H E W R L E
W Y Y T I T S E C S O U A A
H B P N I Y V N I L U S X T
B O A G B V G O N X E J A M
G L R U Y W E B I H M S T E
T D E M M J L R L U E M I N
A F H E O I R M C N D P O T
F Z T U A N I K S G I Q N H
R E F L E X E M J E C T E G
D O C T O R V S T R I H M I
F R A C T U R E Q V N S D E
P H A R M A C Y A K E M Q H
```

ACTIVE
HEIGHT
CLINIC
DOCTOR
PHARMACY
FRACTURE
HUNGER
HABIT
HORMONES
BONES

MEDICINE
MUSCLES
SKIN
POSTURE
REFLEX
RELAXATION
THERAPY
TREATMENT
VIRUS

37 - Adjetivos #2

```
C  I  T  A  M  A  R  D  S  S  E  E  C  I
R  G  N  O  R  T  S  I  A  E  P  V  X  X
E  F  O  O  D  N  D  D  L  D  K  I  E  U
A  A  R  M  G  A  U  E  T  I  G  T  C  L
T  M  M  P  R  G  O  V  Y  B  N  C  N  Y
I  O  A  I  D  E  R  I  T  L  I  U  A  H
V  U  L  B  A  L  P  T  D  E  T  D  T  T
E  S  Y  Z  X  E  G  P  T  C  S  O  U  L
R  E  S  P  O  N  S  I  B  L  E  R  R  A
N  F  L  P  N  V  M  R  H  U  R  P  A  E
F  R  E  S  H  E  K  C  W  E  E  D  L  H
F  M  D  R  Y  N  W  S  Y  H  T  G  Y  F
C  C  I  H  A  A  H  E  W  M  N  T  D  D
C  T  P  Z  S  H  T  D  I  U  I  D  J  F
```

TIRED	NATURAL
EDIBLE	NORMAL
CREATIVE	NEW
DESCRIPTIVE	PROUD
DRAMATIC	SPICY
ELEGANT	PRODUCTIVE
FAMOUS	RESPONSIBLE
FRESH	SALTY
STRONG	HEALTHY
INTERESTING	DRY

38 - Cuerpo Humano

```
L Q M O O F L F X Q H R W Y
C V T H O F M H C N Y A E R
H H S E X X O W T K C E N C
I A G C V N G F H D E C W D
N H E A R T L S E Y E A E K
G I L K X H J G A B E F R N
E L K N A G B F D L S W E E
Q U N S T U V R B L O O D E
H B Y A X M B E A D N B L U
E R P C U O R G B I P L U G
E H E S Q U N N H M N E O N
P V U G D T L I W A I Z H O
Z S D Z C H G F T V G D S T
T C T K X V W E Y A Z I A M
```

CHIN	TONGUE
MOUTH	HAND
HEAD	NOSE
FACE	EYE
BRAIN	EAR
ELBOW	SKIN
HEART	LEG
NECK	KNEE
FINGER	BLOOD
SHOULDER	ANKLE

39 - Ciencia

```
P M P C L I M A T E D S D H
L I A O R G A N I S M A Z A
A N R E V O L U T I O N T T
N E T S C I E N T I S T A A
T R I D O H T E M Z D D P V
S A C I H R W D T O Y J G P
B L L A C I M E H C T C A F
P S E C L C S Z F U I A T Y
E H S H W J L L F A V I C E
R O Y R O T A R O B A L Q N
U K R S F O S S I L R G C W
T N E M I R E P X E G Z J U
A S E L U C E L O M Q J Y R
N Y K V S I S E H T O P Y H
```

ATOM
SCIENTIST
CLIMATE
DATA
EVOLUTION
EXPERIMENT
PHYSICS
FOSSIL
GRAVITY
FACT

HYPOTHESIS
LABORATORY
METHOD
MINERALS
MOLECULES
NATURE
ORGANISM
PARTICLES
PLANTS
CHEMICAL

40 - Restaurante #2

```
Z P F P S B L A D L U U J W
Y X R N A T O N E K A C U N
X R U K L V X H L W S O C W
Q V I P A W Z T I A M A R S
S R T H D X S E C I P S L W
B E V E R A G E I T G F R T
M N C U F I E C O E F N Q C
H N D I O G Z R U R W N L I
F I S H R H G Z S O A O T J
S D G C K N C Q C W T O I E
O Q G N V R E Z I T E P P A
U M E U C H A I R P R S M Z
P S E L B A T E G E V J Z I
M O I V P B P E O B Q X H L
```

WATER
LUNCH
APPETIZER
BEVERAGE
WAITER
DINNER
SPOON
DELICIOUS
SALAD
SPICES

FRUIT
ICE
EGGS
CAKE
FISH
SALT
CHAIR
SOUP
FORK
VEGETABLES

41 - Profesiones #1

```
A M B A S S A D O R W A A H
C O A C H H J R R C L A T U
P S Y C H O L O G I S T T N
A G F M M W L T P M A B O T
S T E S R U N C L U S A R E
H B H O E M Z O U S T N N R
O E L L R S D M I R K E E E
P G X Y E O Y Y B C O E Y C
S I K N W T G Y E I N R G N
O Z A Y E I E I R A O Y C A
V T Z N J D R M S N M C I D
B E G X I E K U E T E F H D
Z M N C X S D H E M R C O E
F K U T Z W T M B Z H A T L
```

ATTORNEY   NURSE
ASTRONOMER   COACH
ATHLETE   PLUMBER
DANCER   GEOLOGIST
BANKER   JEWELER
HUNTER   MUSICIAN
DOCTOR   PIANIST
EDITOR   PSYCHOLOGIST
AMBASSADOR

42 - Geometría

```
R B T E D I A M E T E R V H
H O R I Z O N T A L H E E E
P A R A L L E L U Z E B R I
N O I S N E M I D Y Z M T G
X C B S Y M M E T R Y U I H
D S N A I D E M C L E N C T
S E G M E N T X V S V Q A D
U L L L D O T A Q U O F L X
N G F G G I Y H C L I P B H
U N X I N T N W E V R U C N
Q A J D E A V R K O C P I C
K I B Q B U P U U D R D G Z
H R U R D Q T R O Z E Y O O
P T Q U G E C A F R U S L J
```

HEIGHT	MEDIAN
ANGLE	NUMBER
CURVE	PARALLEL
DIAMETER	SEGMENT
DIMENSION	SYMMETRY
EQUATION	SURFACE
HORIZONTAL	THEORY
LOGIC	TRIANGLE
MASS	VERTICAL

43 - Baile

```
R T T M T J J O Y F U L M W
Y H H R O V I S U A L M F M
F F Y A A V J U M P Y P C G
X F N T H D E R U T S O P P
B O D Y H R I M E R E F V A
W Q U L J M L T E C A R G R
D H T A X G D R I N M Z J T
C L A S S I C A L O T C P N
I L A R U T L U C E N H W E
S R I A C U L T U R E A Y R
U Y M E D A C A M W H N L E
M G I H E M O T I O N S Q G
O F Q E V I S S E R P X E D
C H O R E O G R A P H Y Q M
```

ACADEMY
JOYFUL
ART
CLASSICAL
CHOREOGRAPHY
BODY
CULTURE
CULTURAL
EMOTION
REHEARSAL

EXPRESSIVE
GRACE
MOVEMENT
MUSIC
POSTURE
RHYTHM
JUMP
PARTNER
TRADITIONAL
VISUAL

44 - Matemáticas

```
A P E R P E N D I C U L A R
F N A T R I A N G L E D D F
P O G R D D N J T D R E I R
A I R L I I W W T Y E C P A
E T A N E T A B Z S H I A C
E A D O O S H M D T P M R T
L U I G H L Z M E M S A A I
G Q U Y Z Z X I E T M L L O
N E S L V D L E K T E E L N
A G E O M E T R Y I I R E W
T K D P V O L U M E T C L Z
C I R C U M F E R E N C E Y
E P A R A L L E L O G R A M
R W E X P O N E N T W I K X
```

ARITHMETIC	GEOMETRY
ANGLES	PARALLEL
CIRCUMFERENCE	PARALLELOGRAM
DECIMAL	PERPENDICULAR
DIAMETER	POLYGON
EQUATION	RADIUS
SPHERE	RECTANGLE
EXPONENT	TRIANGLE
FRACTION	VOLUME

45 - Restaurante #1

```
C R H G T M B M H G L I P C
H E E S K F E R F Y D N L A
I S D S U N D A E O Q G A S
C E B E C U A S T A H R T H
K R D R B O W L C S D E E I
E V N T R E S S E D O D W E
N A X I A L L E R G Y I T R
G T A A K P C C D K N E E K
L I S W D P H I A C A N K I
N O P T O E A T Y W G T N T
E N I L O D C N P J A S I C
M O C S F E C O F F E E F H
Y Q Y J M E N U A G L R E E
G B J C T Y T L V B G P F N
```

ALLERGY
COFFEE
CASHIER
WAITRESS
MEAT
KITCHEN
TO EAT
FOOD
KNIFE
INGREDIENTS

MENU
BREAD
SPICY
PLATE
CHICKEN
DESSERT
RESERVATION
SAUCE
NAPKIN
BOWL

46 - Profesiones #2

```
P  T  R  E  P  I  L  O  T  P  B  I  D  X
H  S  E  N  V  U  F  P  F  H  S  N  E  U
I  I  H  A  Y  H  R  L  A  Y  U  V  N  J
L  U  C  I  C  S  E  V  S  S  R  E  T  O
O  G  R  R  P  H  N  N  T  I  G  N  I  U
S  N  A  A  G  A  E  U  R  C  E  T  S  R
O  I  E  R  V  F  D  R  O  I  O  O  T  N
P  L  S  B  P  V  R  E  N  A  N  R  P  A
H  H  E  I  C  Z  A  A  A  N  Z  B  A  L
E  W  R  L  Y  J  G  P  U  B  H  B  I  I
R  E  H  P  A  R  G  O  T  O  H  P  N  S
I  L  L  U  S  T  R  A  T  O  R  H  T  T
B  I  O  L  O  G  I  S  T  L  T  C  E  O
Y  D  E  T  E  C  T  I  V  E  N  D  R  M
```

ASTRONAUT	INVENTOR
LIBRARIAN	RESEARCHER
BIOLOGIST	GARDENER
SURGEON	LINGUIST
DENTIST	PHYSICIAN
DETECTIVE	JOURNALIST
PHILOSOPHER	PILOT
PHOTOGRAPHER	PAINTER
ILLUSTRATOR	TEACHER

47 - Senderismo

```
P  S  T  O  N  E  S  B  X  C  Y  B  S  U
E  R  U  T  A  N  U  D  D  L  I  W  U  L
M  S  E  D  I  U  G  U  Y  I  F  E  M  B
N  F  R  P  Y  Y  Y  R  V  F  Y  I  M  P
G  D  S  L  A  M  I  N  A  F  S  F  I  A
H  W  H  L  N  R  K  I  E  R  T  U  T  R
W  A  T  E  R  M  A  A  H  G  L  E  N  K
M  K  S  N  L  A  S  T  O  O  B  T  O  S
K  C  L  Z  B  P  G  N  I  P  M  A  C  K
B  F  C  H  A  T  C  U  N  O  Z  M  E  H
M  O  S  Q  U  I  T  O  E  S  N  I  Y  E
Z  W  A  R  Y  D  V  M  D  R  B  L  V  O
T  I  R  E  D  J  E  Z  A  J  B  C  F  X
K  D  O  R  I  E  N  T  A  T  I  O  N  E
```

CLIFF	MOUNTAIN
WATER	MOSQUITOES
ANIMALS	NATURE
BOOTS	ORIENTATION
CAMPING	PARKS
TIRED	HEAVY
CLIMATE	STONES
SUMMIT	PREPARATION
GUIDES	WILD
MAP	SUN

48 - Naturaleza

```
H F J W J F F J T I O F G S
C H O N E T S E R O F O K H
I D N G M E U B O I A L M E
M C O V I T A L P Y M I O L
A N I M A L S R I S D A Q T
N W S P Q C W G C O E G Z E
Y A O D T E L R A M S E B R
D Y R E V I R O L F E K E C
Z R E I C A L G U P R Z A U
P E A C E F U L H D T R U T
B W Y R A U T C N A S N T W
I E S E R E N E V Y L P Y I
D V E S S Q Q A R C T I C L
P G C S V M K N R O Y O N D
```

BEES
ANIMALS
ARCTIC
BEAUTY
FOREST
DESERT
DYNAMIC
EROSION
FOLIAGE
GLACIER

FOG
CLOUDS
PEACEFUL
SHELTER
RIVER
WILD
SANCTUARY
SERENE
TROPICAL
VITAL

49 - Conduciendo

```
S  C  F  T  E  E  R  T  S  J  T  P  O  Z
U  A  W  W  R  E  G  N  A  D  R  E  H  Z
B  T  F  C  Q  A  C  A  R  A  U  D  Y  X
A  R  L  E  U  F  F  X  E  P  C  E  D  B
C  G  Q  G  T  K  V  F  C  E  K  S  A  M
C  N  U  A  J  Y  V  K  I  L  L  T  D  E
I  E  S  R  O  T  O  M  L  C  I  R  L  N
D  A  W  A  S  M  B  S  O  Y  C  I  J  F
E  P  B  G  L  D  A  E  P  C  E  A  N  A
N  T  U  N  N  E  L  K  D  R  N  N  T  D
T  U  L  L  S  R  G  A  S  O  S  T  L  E
M  S  P  E  E  D  U  R  C  T  E  Q  X  W
Z  A  B  I  P  X  H  B  K  O  X  T  Q  P
R  W  P  C  H  H  G  D  V  M  L  L  C  Z
```

ACCIDENT	MAP
BUS	MOTORCYCLE
STREET	MOTOR
TRUCK	PEDESTRIAN
CAR	DANGER
FUEL	POLICE
BRAKES	SAFETY
GARAGE	TRAFFIC
GAS	TUNNEL
LICENSE	SPEED

50 - Ballet

```
V  K  J  X  D  X  R  P  C  P  P  I  B  L
C  R  O  B  H  D  P  R  O  M  U  S  I  C
M  H  M  J  D  C  L  A  M  L  A  S  A  D
S  N  O  S  S  E  L  C  P  H  P  F  U  A
B  Q  U  R  J  N  I  T  O  W  P  S  D  N
A  A  P  S  E  H  K  I  S  Y  L  R  I  C
J  I  L  W  C  O  S  C  E  G  A  H  E  E
O  V  K  L  M  Y  G  E  R  L  U  Y  N  R
E  S  M  E  E  S  A  R  R  A  S  T  C  S
S  T  Y  L  E  R  B  M  A  U  E  H  E  C
W  H  I  H  D  F  I  S  E  P  T  M  E  N
M  U  S  C  L  E  S  N  Q  J  H  S  I  D
A  R  T  I  S  T  I  C  A  L  F  Y  E  V
I  N  T  E  N  S  I  T  Y  B  O  D  W  G
```

APPLAUSE	GESTURE
ARTISTIC	SKILL
AUDIENCE	INTENSITY
BALLERINA	LESSONS
DANCERS	MUSCLES
COMPOSER	MUSIC
CHOREOGRAPHY	PRACTICE
STYLE	RHYTHM

51 - Fuerza y Gravedad

```
D  P  M  A  G  N  I  T  U  D  E  K  H  D
D  I  L  L  P  R  O  P  E  R  T  I  E  S
Y  S  S  A  A  P  H  Y  S  I  C  S  Y  T
N  P  I  T  N  S  L  K  R  U  Q  M  Y  M
A  E  X  J  A  E  R  U  S  S  E  R  P  E
M  E  A  N  O  T  E  E  M  R  K  W  C
I  D  O  O  U  M  C  S  V  C  E  W  Q  H
C  W  E  I  G  H  T  E  U  I  T  C  H  A
E  R  G  S  T  I  M  E  N  M  N  W  M  N
M  A  G  N  E  T  I  S  M  P  E  U  P  I
O  R  Z  A  N  D  K  T  J  A  C  O  N  C
I  C  O  P  Y  R  E  V  O  C  S  I  D  S
W  Q  F  X  V  K  U  W  K  T  I  B  R  O
O  Q  F  E  F  R  I  C  T  I  O  N  M  R
```

CENTER
DISCOVERY
DYNAMIC
DISTANCE
AXIS
EXPANSION
PHYSICS
FRICTION
IMPACT
MAGNETISM

MAGNITUDE
MECHANICS
ORBIT
WEIGHT
PLANETS
PRESSURE
PROPERTIES
TIME
UNIVERSAL
SPEED

52 - Aventura

```
K K J S O V B K Y Q J I E D
M E E Y R A R E N I T I N E
S L Y G H Y V R A B K V T S
D A N G E R O U S U S I H T
N U O K M V R J M A T E U I
E S H F G J N R B C B Y S N
I U C U W G E E R T R T I A
R N C H A N C E W I A E A T
F U N A T U R E M V V F S I
E X C U R S I O N I E A M O
T R A V E L S U Q T R S J N
I X I G I X S Y D Y Y R H B
F R S U R P R I S I N G D T
P R E P A R A T I O N T Q K
```

ACTIVITY
JOY
FRIENDS
BEAUTY
DESTINATION
ENTHUSIASM
EXCURSION
UNUSUAL
ITINERARY

NATURE
NEW
CHANCE
DANGEROUS
PREPARATION
SAFETY
SURPRISING
BRAVERY
TRAVELS

53 - Pájaros

```
F E S O O G E F Y O D S Z P
N L N W K G D S S W Z T D A
K G A X D E G C O C A O D R
A A W M S N E D X W O R B R
O E S W I C U C K O O K C O
A O W A G N S P A R R O W T
X Y P N O E G I P I Y A W C
H K B A C K Y O X H I H V H
O E L C R P E N G U I N G
Y Y R U O I H C I R T S O U
I W H O W H B A O F R K L L
K H N T N C V M W U K Y M L
C M H S K Y M L Z K C U D E
P E L I C A N G C A G X R T
```

OSTRICH
EAGLE
STORK
SWAN
CUCKOO
CROW
FLAMINGO
GOOSE
HERON
GULL

SPARROW
HAWK
EGG
PARROT
PIGEON
DUCK
PELICAN
PENGUIN
CHICKEN
TOUCAN

54 - Geografía

```
H T R O N C W M Z M H C L T
D N X J M L F Y F O E M O E
M E S J A E S Q W U M E N R
C N A W P Z V W E N I R G R
L I L R E V I R S T S I I I
A T T A E T E H T A P D T T
S N A Y D G C H C I H I U O
V O O M U X I O X N E A D R
H C V Z T W X O U Z R N E Y
W H D I I D B T N N E E X R
G J I H T U O S X K T W C X
G O Z Q A I S L A N D R T S
I O W D L R O W B H S J Y A
L H A X A L T I T U D E L H
```

ALTITUDE
ATLAS
CITY
CONTINENT
HEMISPHERE
ISLAND
LATITUDE
LONGITUDE
MAP
SEA

MERIDIAN
MOUNTAIN
WORLD
NORTH
WEST
COUNTRY
REGION
RIVER
SOUTH
TERRITORY

55 - Música

```
M U X N A I C I S U M L W W
S E A C A R Y H J C N J V E
I C L R M O N C O V C O G S
N L A O T N E M U R T S N I
G A C A D P N O K N U J I V
E S O Q A Y O S P N E S D O
R S V J L N H D S E K W R R
C I W I L O P M E T R M O P
S C T U A M O L R U F A C M
I A H I B R R A L B U M E I
N L Z W Z A C I T E O P R I
G K U M Y H I M U S I C A L
L I N X C R M R H Y T H M U
H A R M O N I C Z Z C H V S
```

HARMONY	INSTRUMENT
HARMONIC	MELODY
ALBUM	MICROPHONE
BALLAD	MUSICAL
SINGER	MUSICIAN
SING	OPERA
CLASSICAL	POETIC
CHORUS	RHYTHM
RECORDING	TEMPO
IMPROVISE	VOCAL

56 - Actividades

```
G Y H P A R G O T O H P H I
A K E A I S C I M A R E C N
M L L I K S R I B W M S I T
E Y G N I D A E R H M E G E
S C O T C H F P H U L W A R
Z Y T I V I T C A N B I M E
V Q G N I H S I F T E N N S
L R R G W Q T T O I R G Z T
W E J H A X L W F N U A V S
G N I N E D R A G G S J H O
J Q E S N O I T A X A L E R
Y X R S U P U Z Z L E S B D
N B Z M T R S Z L T L U G N
H I K I N G E G V S P T I C
```

ACTIVITY
ART
CRAFTS
HUNTING
CERAMICS
SEWING
PHOTOGRAPHY
SKILL
INTERESTS
GARDENING

GAMES
READING
MAGIC
LEISURE
FISHING
PAINTING
PLEASURE
RELAXATION
PUZZLES
HIKING

57 - Instrumentos Musicales

```
F  U  W  S  M  C  P  N  M  L  X  D  U  K
L  D  W  K  A  B  R  D  W  C  U  S  W  E
U  N  C  Q  R  R  A  C  Y  E  D  M  U  N
T  O  E  U  I  A  H  N  U  D  E  R  V  O
E  O  L  T  M  O  T  V  J  B  N  H  U  B
H  S  L  E  B  J  N  I  L  O  I  V  M  M
G  S  O  P  A  H  P  M  U  R  R  A  A  O
H  A  R  M  O  N  I  C  A  G  U  G  N  R
E  B  T  U  N  R  T  A  H  N  O  C  D  T
L  X  S  R  A  R  V  M  W  O  B  O  O  I
W  F  X  T  I  V  J  R  S  G  M  B  L  J
S  A  X  O  P  H  O  N  E  D  A  O  I  P
P  E  R  C  U  S  S  I  O  N  T  E  N  Q
W  F  E  C  L  A  R  I  N  E  T  P  C  H
```

HARMONICA	OBOE
HARP	TAMBOURINE
BANJO	PERCUSSION
CLARINET	PIANO
BASSOON	SAXOPHONE
FLUTE	DRUM
GONG	TROMBONE
GUITAR	TRUMPET
MANDOLIN	VIOLIN
MARIMBA	CELLO

58 - Mascotas

```
D  C  Q  Z  R  S  Y  T  A  C  U  Z  J  G
O  O  D  R  A  Z  I  L  U  U  W  Q  N  V
G  L  N  P  B  Y  C  T  U  R  P  F  B  M
P  L  H  A  B  K  H  U  U  P  T  J  K  O
B  A  H  S  I  F  O  O  D  A  W  L  U  U
C  R  Q  T  T  L  W  N  Z  R  X  I  E  S
V  O  I  A  S  Y  A  T  C  R  T  A  P  E
P  U  P  P  Y  Y  T  O  E  O  G  T  F  S
N  K  Y  B  O  D  E  W  N  T  A  O  G  V
P  W  I  L  V  R  R  E  T  S  M  A  H  C
W  W  W  R  E  E  E  K  F  W  W  F  Z  O
N  X  N  T  J  A  E  H  T  A  G  A  M  W
U  J  A  H  K  A  S  S  F  L  S  D  P  M
R  X  C  F  X  C  J  H  Y  C  V  Q  V  P
```

WATER	HAMSTER
GOAT	LIZARD
PUPPY	PARROT
TAIL	PAWS
COLLAR	DOG
FOOD	FISH
RABBIT	MOUSE
LEASH	TURTLE
CLAWS	COW
CAT	

59 - Formas

```
R Q D Z Q V T R I A N G L E
A E D I S D L C B E O Y P W
X R C S G A L O B R E P Y H
D E W T W F E R N X B R R U
U H R H A S L N E J U A A T
K P P E C N B E M L C R M C
Y S T B D M G R G C C C I R
C O N E A G N L H Y U R D J
M Y R Y M M E J E L R L I B
E L L I P S E S R I V I Y C
R U E W Q I W O A N E N E U
R H A C T R R V U D Z E Y Y
X X Y Z N P E A Q E L A O I
P O L Y G O N L S R W S G F
```

ARC	CORNER
EDGES	HYPERBOLA
CYLINDER	SIDE
CIRCLE	LINE
CONE	OVAL
SQUARE	PYRAMID
CUBE	POLYGON
CURVE	PRISM
ELLIPSE	RECTANGLE
SPHERE	TRIANGLE

60 - Flores

```
X N Z U U D X C M T L L X C
U K Y A T A C A A U I A O Z
Y X M C D F R L G L L V F V
R H O H G F N E N I Y E B O
T E U Q U O B N O P N N J R
D H V T J D S D L J O D L C
V M Y O B I U U I U E E I H
H C J M L L C L A P P R L I
W L O Q U C S A R D O I A D
G A R D E N I A O D U P C X
P T Y V I A B Y S I A D P V
H E A H P K I H E C A S O Y
I P W R Y Y H J A S M I N E
D A N D E L I O N Q U H O Z
```

POPPY

CALENDULA

DANDELION

GARDENIA

HIBISCUS

JASMINE

LAVENDER

LILAC

LILY

MAGNOLIA

DAISY

DAFFODIL

ORCHID

PEONY

PETAL

BOUQUET

ROSE

CLOVER

TULIP

61 - Astronomía

```
T U A N O R T S A O U S O V
R E M O N O R T S A N U Q L
P T L M E T E O R T I P T S
L I J E S P I L C E V E P K
Z L X K S P H X T K E R L Y
J L R F D C X N G C R N A C
K E R U Q N O I N O S O N O
H T R A E S N P G R E V E S
U A B J Y T I V E A M A T M
D S I P W G U C N C L O A O
W M K B Z D Q S H L K A O S
M V P R Y B E R W V O L X N
R A D I A T I O N K B Y W Y
A S T E R O I D P H Y Q O I
```

ASTEROID
ASTRONAUT
ASTRONOMER
SKY
ROCKET
COSMOS
ECLIPSE
EQUINOX
GALAXY

MOON
METEOR
PLANET
RADIATION
SATELLITE
SUPERNOVA
TELESCOPE
EARTH
UNIVERSE

62 - Paisajes

```
P E V A C D A E A N G Q V D
A E S I S A O N A C L O V R
W T N T L Q N X D N A L S I
R A C I U B E A C H C D Q L
I R T Y N A O A N K I E Z L
V D X E G S R A O C E S A O
E N D O R S U Y O Q R E F S
R U G H E F S L G N O R S W
E T N F B M A S A T P T L A
S M U S E Y E L L A V Q E M
Y D K O C T V D L G A C W P
E M J N I A T N U O M J E Y
G O Z H J K I O D S U P A Q
L A K E P P I U F E M N P I
```

WATERFALL	SEA
CAVE	MOUNTAIN
DESERT	OASIS
ESTUARY	SWAMP
GEYSER	PENINSULA
GLACIER	BEACH
ICEBERG	RIVER
ISLAND	TUNDRA
LAKE	VALLEY
LAGOON	VOLCANO

63 - Días y Meses

```
T X D S S K Y S N A Y U Y K
D K Q U A V A I O I V D X Y
V S M N T W D M V P Y H L A
M D O D U L S W E N U J R D
V Y N A R R E B M E T P E S
H R D Y D A N B B C D C F R
T A A L A E D D E W E E K U
N U Y U Y Y E N R C C B F H
O N E J Z B W B E D X U R T
M A H S D Y E G B L H L I Y
J J E Z D N D W O B A R D X
M D V N G A J J T J T C A N
R A P R I L Y Z C Y N H Y C
A U G U S T G H O A Q H X Z
```

APRIL
AUGUST
YEAR
CALENDAR
SUNDAY
JANUARY
THURSDAY
JULY
JUNE
MONDAY

TUESDAY
MONTH
WEDNESDAY
NOVEMBER
OCTOBER
SATURDAY
WEEK
SEPTEMBER
FRIDAY

64 - Jardinería

```
F A E L Q O B N N V S A E B
S L U S M J D L X A O E X O
E Z O K I X T X O W I W O T
A Z D R A H C R O S L O T A
S H T N A W A T E R S E I N
O S Q F J L C J M A A O C I
N E M O I S T U R E M J M C
A E C R E D I B L E E S Z A
L D L J C O N T A I N E R L
Q S I B O U Q U E T R I D I
V U M F O Q R H K H Z C G I
E G A I L O F A O B T E V L
X H T K U J Y M Y S A P Z H
I Y E C O M P O S T E S C M
```

WATER	FLORAL
BOTANICAL	FOLIAGE
CLIMATE	LEAF
EDIBLE	ORCHARD
COMPOST	MOISTURE
CONTAINER	HOSE
SPECIES	BOUQUET
SEASONAL	SEEDS
EXOTIC	DIRT
BLOSSOM	SOIL

65 - Chocolate

```
A F D L E M A R A C R P R W
C R A N Q X X E R I E O C H
A Z T V Z Z O T O P C W C T
L Y N I O A N T Z O I D O A
O Z A F S R A I I A P E C S
R D D L G A I B Y C E R O T
I E I A X G N T U A L A N E
E L X V I U I A E C M Y U Q
S I O O P S X N L Y H R T U
V C I R R W K F E O C N E A
Z I T N E I D E R G N I E L
B O N L A R O M A L U N W I
V U A L E O D T D G X Q S T
J S T U N A E P D T S L N Y
```

BITTER
ANTIOXIDANT
AROMA
ARTISANAL
SUGAR
PEANUTS
CACAO
QUALITY
CALORIES
CARAMEL

COCONUT
DELICIOUS
SWEET
EXOTIC
FAVORITE
TASTE
INGREDIENT
POWDER
RECIPE
FLAVOR

66 - Barbacoas

```
F  T  E  T  V  X  C  K  D  O  C  O  X  P
A  O  H  Z  E  F  H  R  O  H  U  N  V  Q
M  M  C  K  G  Q  I  E  S  E  V  I  N  K
I  A  H  H  E  B  L  P  R  E  W  O  U  J
L  T  I  H  T  F  D  P  O  D  B  N  A  R
Y  O  C  O  A  G  R  E  M  M  U  S  V  N
V  E  K  X  B  E  E  P  S  Q  H  K  J  R
V  S  E  K  L  C  N  D  Z  M  N  O  F  R
W  L  N  J  E  S  D  I  X  S  D  T  T  N
Y  Z  M  T  S  Z  P  N  S  D  A  L  A  S
A  M  U  S  I  C  S  N  R  I  I  U  W  W
G  A  M  E  S  U  N  E  S  A  L  T  C  S
H  U  N  G  E  R  R  R  R  G  R  I  L  L  E
D  E  F  R  M  G  U  F  L  U  N  C  H  G
```

LUNCH	MUSIC
HOT	CHILDREN
ONIONS	GRILL
DINNER	PEPPER
KNIVES	CHICKEN
SALADS	SALT
FAMILY	SAUCE
FRUIT	TOMATOES
HUNGER	SUMMER
GAMES	VEGETABLES

67 - Ropa

```
P  J  E  W  E  L  R  Y  F  C  A  Q  O  X
X  A  B  E  L  T  A  H  A  O  R  V  I  K
V  O  J  Q  U  E  H  B  S  E  V  O  L  G
X  D  T  A  C  K  O  R  H  S  E  O  H  S
L  K  U  N  M  C  E  A  I  T  C  Q  U  M
Z  T  A  O  C  A  F  C  O  N  A  A  T  K
D  R  E  S  S  J  S  E  N  A  L  H  R  X
S  I  S  S  S  D  I  L  U  P  K  O  I  F
W  H  U  B  A  H  U  E  A  R  C  O  K  F
E  S  O  B  F  N  J  T  C  F  E  S  S  L
A  G  L  M  Q  M  D  E  P  N  N  P  S  N
T  F  B  N  A  Q  X  A  A  P  R  O  N  P
E  B  X  V  G  O  Y  S  L  T  T  V  F  W
R  B  W  L  B  N  A  C  J  S  K  E  B  I
```

COAT	JEWELRY
BLOUSE	FASHION
SCARF	PANTS
SHIRT	PAJAMAS
JACKET	BRACELET
BELT	SANDALS
NECKLACE	HAT
APRON	SWEATER
SKIRT	DRESS
GLOVES	SHOE

68 - Meditación

```
P  V  V  E  K  G  K  C  H  T  Y  U  M  O
O  A  V  M  K  I  N  B  C  N  U  T  I  B
S  N  N  O  I  T  N  E  T  T  A  R  N  S
T  G  E  T  M  M  V  D  M  M  O  A  D  E
U  N  W  I  T  L  A  T  N  E  M  X  P  R
R  I  V  O  Y  A  Q  Y  V  E  T  F  E  V
E  H  D  N  H  C  I  S  U  M  S  Z  P  A
N  T  K  S  D  F  G  R  K  F  J  S  J  T
Y  A  P  E  R  S  P  E  C  T  I  V  E  I
F  E  T  G  R  A  T  I  T  U  D  E  V  O
O  R  A  U  Z  H  C  L  A  R  I  T  Y  N
O  B  F  N  R  T  H  O  U  G  H  T  S  R
S  K  A  T  N  E  M  E  V  O  M  Z  M  F
G  B  P  E  A  C  E  S  I  L  E  N  C  E
```

ATTENTION	MUSIC
KINDNESS	NATURE
CALM	OBSERVATION
CLARITY	PEACE
EMOTIONS	THOUGHTS
GRATITUDE	PERSPECTIVE
MENTAL	POSTURE
MIND	BREATHING
MOVEMENT	SILENCE

69 - Café

```
L C F D F R B P H S W E X C
I R I B A H F G Y R U S P M
Q E L K M L Q D Y N E G X T
U A T G O O R Y T E I R A V
I M E S R A R R K P V D B R
D N R F A W P N L S S Y D O
P U C I D I C A I K S Y B V
W R E T T I B W M N I F E A
E N I E F F A C V O G O V L
H I E C W A T E R D D M E F
C G G D E T S A O R G Y R J
B I G R I N D D R U F Q A U
W R F H E M I B L A C K G H
R O F O N P Q X T Z G Q E P
```

WATER	MILK
BITTER	LIQUID
AROMA	MORNING
ROASTED	GRIND
SUGAR	BLACK
ACIDIC	ORIGIN
BEVERAGE	PRICE
CAFFEINE	FLAVOR
CREAM	CUP
FILTER	VARIETY

70 - Libros

```
E I E N R P M A C C H L R S
A N P O E D S U O R O M U H
M V D V A L D Q N S L T U U
H E T E D M E Y T I L A U D
I N O L E Y R R E Y M L T U
S T R P R R U O X X W S R N
T I O E W A T T A R E A A
O V H I L R N S V C I R G R
R E T E K E E I D P T I I R
I K U N Q T V A B A T E C A
C S A P F I D A N G E S N T
A U I L H L A J N E N A W O
L C F E B K Q Y R T E O P R
C O L L E C T I O N Z H C C
```

AUTHOR
ADVENTURE
COLLECTION
CONTEXT
DUALITY
WRITTEN
STORY
HISTORICAL
HUMOROUS
INVENTIVE

READER
LITERARY
NARRATOR
NOVEL
PAGE
RELEVANT
POEM
POETRY
SERIES
TRAGIC

71 - Los Medios de Comunicación

```
B  C  F  A  T  T  I  T  U  D  E  S  P  P
V  T  O  A  E  D  U  C  A  T  I  O  N  U
M  A  Y  M  C  E  D  I  T  I  O  N  O  B
L  O  Y  K  M  T  F  U  N  D  I  N  G  L
P  T  S  R  N  U  S  W  A  Y  A  C  K  I
R  H  F  O  Z  G  N  O  I  N  I  P  O  C
A  K  O  W  L  E  N  I  L  N  O  B  L  Y
D  L  A  T  I  G  I  D  C  R  V  R  G  R
I  J  Y  E  O  O  B  T  L  A  C  O  L  T
O  Z  E  N  R  S  G  C  A  X  T  V  Z  S
C  O  M  M  E  R  C  I  A  L  N  I  V  U
I  N  T  E  L  L  E  C  T  U  A  L  O  D
M  A  G  A  Z  I  N  E  S  B  G  H  T  N
N  E  W  S  P  A  P  E  R  S  A  Q  A  I
```

ATTITUDES
COMMERCIAL
COMMUNICATION
DIGITAL
EDITION
EDUCATION
ONLINE
FUNDING
PHOTOS
FACTS

INDUSTRY
INTELLECTUAL
LOCAL
OPINION
NEWSPAPERS
PUBLIC
RADIO
NETWORK
MAGAZINES

72 - Nutrición

```
C W U Q N U T R I E N T H I
F A A E U M M V D U W E E V
E C R L W A U N I X O T A Q
R E O B S E L W E Q A I L D
M R V I O M I I T W Z T T I
E E A D S H Q G T M J E H G
N A L E N F Y V H Y X P Y E
T L F D I P G D I T P P N S
A S M E E S E I R O L A C T
T S B I T T E R K A X W P I
I J T T O A C N S U T I B O
O H S V R M U E U S A E Q N
N R G Y P Z A J I P C I S C
H E A L T H S V I T A M I N
```

BITTER   NUTRIENT
APPETITE   WEIGHT
QUALITY   PROTEINS
CALORIES   FLAVOR
CARBOHYDRATES   SAUCE
CEREALS   HEALTH
EDIBLE   HEALTHY
DIET   TOXIN
DIGESTION   VITAMIN
FERMENTATION

73 - Edificios

```
C E S U P E R M A R K E T T
Z W L L A B O R A T O R Y H
B C Y T I S R E V I N U E E
E M B A S S Y M U S E U M A
P R Q A B A C X A L L H H T
K A H O V J C S O S G O O E
C F L X V P P K C D G T S R
T I B U B L Y F O H A E P S
O T N E M T R A P A R L I T
W P R E J A O G Z R A O T A
E R A P M O T X I G G O A D
R J B D K A C F O D E H L I
O B S E R V A T O R Y C L U
H O S T E L F U V T J S C M
```

HOSTEL	FARM
APARTMENT	HOSPITAL
CASTLE	HOTEL
CINEMA	LABORATORY
EMBASSY	MUSEUM
SCHOOL	OBSERVATORY
STADIUM	SUPERMARKET
FACTORY	THEATER
GARAGE	TOWER
BARN	UNIVERSITY

74 - Océano

```
T T S E R C O R A L D Y F W
A I U X L B P E G N O P S I
O S D N A R X T S H R I M P
B J H E A B H S U P O T C O
N T L A S V W Y Z R T S W I
Z W P K R I F O E L T R U T
H S Y Q H K P T E J F L K N
C N J H O B B A L L J P Y I
R L J H K J E L L Y F I S H
A X X Q D V F Y N I H O R P
B L F I S H O W H A L E O L
V R E M V U T E E H D M E O
I O E L Z N R K R H E R P D
P M R O T S E A L G A E G M
```

ALGAE
EEL
REEF
TUNA
WHALE
BOAT
SHRIMP
CRAB
CORAL
DOLPHIN

SPONGE
TIDES
JELLYFISH
OYSTER
FISH
OCTOPUS
SALT
SHARK
STORM
TURTLE

75 - Deporte

```
D O O R V B I S E N O B J K
M A B Q S O H T G N E R T S
I U N P G D C R E X L E N T
W M S C N Y A E T I E N U O
S A T C I S O T E H D D T B
O R L C L N C C L E U U R R
T G D K C E G H H A P R I E
A O T O Y R S I T L G A T A
A R L H C J C N A T T N I T
S P O R T S A G W H X C O H
M E T A B O L I C K U E N E
N A B I L I T Y Y N U K T T
T Q J B T M J Q L Y N O H X
R N K H R S M A X I M I Z E
```

ATHLETE
DANCING
ABILITY
CYCLING
BODY
SPORTS
DIET
COACH
STRETCHING
STRENGTH

BONES
MAXIMIZE
METABOLIC
MUSCLES
TO SWIM
NUTRITION
PROGRAM
ENDURANCE
TO BREATHE
HEALTH

76 - Actividades y Ocio

```
G  C  B  L  J  G  N  I  K  I  H  P  S  B
A  B  P  W  Y  X  O  L  T  O  V  A  O  O
R  A  R  X  Y  R  D  L  O  K  E  I  C  X
D  S  O  E  J  D  R  J  F  B  N  N  C  I
E  E  T  D  L  E  V  A  R  T  L  T  E  N
N  B  O  X  L  A  W  G  Q  R  S  I  R  G
I  A  I  V  A  N  X  N  S  A  W  N  D  N
N  L  C  N  B  Y  U  I  I  V  I  G  I  I
G  L  U  D  T  V  V  P  N  G  M  N  V  F
S  L  E  O  E  Z  V  P  N  G  M  I  I  R
G  Z  C  X  K  R  L  O  E  H  I  P  N  U
G  N  I  H  S  I  F  H  T  B  N  M  G  S
X  H  B  C  A  H  S  S  U  T  G  A  F  P
Y  D  J  C  B  R  A  C  I  N  G  C  K  B
```

ART	GARDENING
BASKETBALL	SWIMMING
BASEBALL	FISHING
BOXING	PAINTING
DIVING	RELAXING
CAMPING	HIKING
RACING	SURFING
SHOPPING	TENNIS
SOCCER	TRAVEL
GOLF	

77 - Ingeniería

```
M  Y  L  E  S  E  I  D  E  C  M  W  S  O
I  A  E  P  J  O  F  T  N  R  T  M  T  E
P  L  V  P  I  H  T  P  E  D  I  E  R  H
L  X  E  H  T  G  N  E  R  T  S  A  U  D
M  L  R  O  T  O  M  Q  G  O  G  C  C  I
K  C  S  I  X  A  H  Q  Y  S  R  E  T  A
A  C  A  L  C  U  L  A  T  I  O  N  U  M
O  N  L  F  R  I  C  T  I  O  N  I  R  E
I  R  G  I  G  Y  Y  F  N  P  X  H  E  T
L  Z  O  L  Q  Q  C  R  K  K  Y  C  I  E
T  R  P  D  E  U  F  U  P  N  Z  A  U  R
G  D  Y  T  I  L  I  B  A  T  S  M  F  G
D  I  A  G  R  A  M  D  I  Y  O  D  M  T
D  I  S  T  R  I  B  U  T  I  O  N  P  E
```

ANGLE	STRUCTURE
CALCULATION	FRICTION
DIAGRAM	STRENGTH
DIAMETER	LIQUID
DIESEL	MACHINE
DISTRIBUTION	MOTOR
AXIS	LEVERS
ENERGY	DEPTH
STABILITY	

78 - Comida #1

```
L X D R Y R R E B W A R T S
O H C A N I P S A M M W U X
N O M E L X U X S I E A K J
I S O U P A I C I L R A G U
O E I Y L D S K L I M N T I
N R P T U R N I P A S U S C
M O N H D A T K Z M U T A E
I Z M X Y E L R A B G F L K
N M N A I P M R C L A T T T
T G C Q N J S F V B R T I G
N F T R S N C A R R O T Q X
Y M J Q J Y I P U V W M L R
S F S G I Q D C E P C K M L
C Q W O O T I V Z V L M S Y
```

GARLIC	STRAWBERRY
BASIL	JUICE
TUNA	MILK
SUGAR	LEMON
CINNAMON	MINT
MEAT	TURNIP
BARLEY	PEAR
ONION	SALT
SALAD	SOUP
SPINACH	CARROT

79 - Antigüedades

```
C  I  X  Q  G  V  E  X  U  W  O  S  K  C
E  N  K  U  A  A  D  N  O  I  T  C  U  A
N  O  R  A  L  L  Q  I  A  P  O  U  C  P
T  I  E  L  L  U  Y  S  P  R  D  L  O  F
U  T  L  I  E  E  D  M  C  I  Y  P  I  A
R  A  E  T  R  E  F  E  Y  C  Q  T  N  U
Y  R  G  Y  Y  V  E  L  C  E  M  U  S  T
C  O  A  T  V  L  I  Y  K  A  X  R  W  H
A  T  N  U  M  X  G  T  R  A  D  E  G  E
X  S  T  G  L  A  U  S  U  N  U  E  D  N
D  E  C  O  R  A  T  I  V  E  R  B  S  T
E  R  U  T  I  N  R  U  F  W  I  E  R  I
I  N  V  E  S  T  M  E  N  T  J  M  T  C
P  G  J  E  W  E  L  R  Y  R  K  C  V  B
```

ART
AUTHENTIC
QUALITY
DECORATIVE
DECADES
ELEGANT
SCULPTURE
STYLE
GALLERY
UNUSUAL

INVESTMENT
JEWELRY
COINS
FURNITURE
PRICE
RESTORATION
CENTURY
AUCTION
VALUE
OLD

80 - Literatura

```
E  C  M  A  S  V  G  C  F  S  U  I  R  I
T  F  O  H  V  E  R  O  H  T  U  A  X  F
O  T  R  M  T  L  Q  M  F  F  X  A  S  F
D  C  M  G  L  Y  H  P  A  R  G  O  I  B
C  E  M  E  H  T  H  A  P  O  D  C  S  A
E  R  S  J  O  S  J  R  O  H  I  O  Y  N
N  R  X  C  F  K  K  I  E  P  A  N  L  A
A  C  Z  O  R  J  P  S  M  A  L  C  A  L
R  H  Y  M  E  I  T  O  H  T  O  L  N  O
P  O  E  T  I  C  P  N  B  E  G  U  A  G
N  O  V  E  L  F  U  T  B  M  U  S  Q  Y
N  A  R  R  A  T  O  R  I  A  E  I  S  L
T  R  A  G  E  D  Y  U  Q  O  N  O  Y  C
J  C  F  I  C  T  I  O  N  O  N  N  H  N
```

ANALOGY	FICTION
ANALYSIS	METAPHOR
ANECDOTE	NARRATOR
AUTHOR	NOVEL
BIOGRAPHY	POEM
COMPARISON	POETIC
CONCLUSION	RHYME
DESCRIPTION	RHYTHM
DIALOGUE	THEME
STYLE	TRAGEDY

81 - Química

```
M U R M B M S P J S A L T R
O P D J N U C L E A R K G E
L E K O O A K E A O D H V A
E Q S N R M D K U T A E H C
C E R U T A R E P M E T T T
U P Z U C C U X H C N M T I
L V A V E I D I U Q I L S O
E S E L L D U R C K L M Y N
F N P D E V F T A K A R L I
E N Z Y M E T D R J K G A S
O X Y G E N Z M B H L L T T
C H L O R I N E O Y A V A C
W E I G H T W O N T H D C A
H Y D R O G E N I K K F T R
```

ALKALINE	ION
ACID	LIQUID
HEAT	METALS
CARBON	MOLECULE
CATALYST	NUCLEAR
CHLORINE	OXYGEN
ELECTRON	WEIGHT
ENZYME	REACTION
GAS	SALT
HYDROGEN	TEMPERATURE

82 - Gobierno

```
X  E  C  N  E  D  N  E  P  E  D  N  I  P
V  O  C  Q  V  R  W  A  L  S  V  W  G  O
J  U  S  T  I  C  E  U  T  X  P  E  J  U
D  E  Q  U  A  L  I  T  Y  I  N  K  B  M
H  I  W  B  H  I  M  K  R  D  O  O  Y  J
I  C  S  T  O  V  E  Y  C  Y  Q  N  L  G
F  W  E  C  Z  I  Y  T  R  L  Y  S  A  E
L  F  J  W  U  C  K  R  E  Z  C  C  I  L
E  E  P  I  H  S  N  E  Z  I  T  I  C  S
O  T  A  R  C  D  S  B  I  A  V  T  I  Y
E  A  O  D  E  T  C  I  R  T  S  I  D  M
M  T  T  S  E  Q  Q  L  O  M  A  L  U  B
G  S  P  U  P  R  Q  H  I  N  L  O  J  O
G  A  D  P  S  N  A  T  I  O  N  P  K  L
```

CITIZENSHIP	JUSTICE
CIVIL	LAW
SPEECH	LIBERTY
DISCUSSION	LEADER
DISTRICT	NATIONAL
STATE	NATION
EQUALITY	POLITICS
INDEPENDENCE	SYMBOL
JUDICIAL	

83 - Creatividad

```
S  A  E  D  I  D  R  A  M  A  T  I  C  I
A  E  I  N  S  P  I  R  A  T  I  O  N  M
R  S  N  I  N  T  U  I  T  I  O  N  I  A
T  K  W  S  Z  Y  Z  R  C  H  B  Z  M  G
I  I  Q  N  A  Y  T  I  R  A  L  C  A  I
S  L  N  O  Y  T  I  D  I  U  L  F  G  N
T  L  U  I  F  I  I  U  Y  V  O  H  E  A
I  T  G  S  D  S  N  O  I  T  O  M  E  T
C  E  V  I  T  N  E  V  N  I  Q  O  O  I
A  T  A  V  O  E  D  N  U  T  P  C  W  O
Z  D  P  A  U  T  V  Q  S  M  F  N  U  N
X  F  Z  Y  F  N  V  I  T  A  L  I  T  Y
A  Y  T  I  C  I  T  N  E  H  T  U  A  W
S  P  O  N  T  A  N  E  O  U  S  J  J  U
```

ARTISTIC   IMAGE
AUTHENTICITY   IMAGINATION
CLARITY   INSPIRATION
DRAMATIC   INTENSITY
EMOTIONS   INTUITION
SPONTANEOUS   INVENTIVE
FLUIDITY   SENSATION
SKILL   VISIONS
IDEAS   VITALITY

84 - Filantropía

```
P  P  E  O  P  L  E  G  G  L  I  J  A  C
R  G  N  E  E  D  Z  G  L  K  K  P  P  H
O  G  E  F  U  N  D  S  X  O  L  A  Y  I
G  R  C  N  Q  A  C  U  Y  P  B  P  M  L
R  O  N  B  E  T  A  N  O  D  E  A  M  D
A  U  A  G  Y  R  O  T  S  I  H  O  L  R
M  P  N  Q  K  F  O  E  Z  U  M  Z  R  E
S  S  I  Y  M  F  Z  S  B  T  C  D  R  N
L  J  F  P  E  W  Y  T  I  R  A  H  C  P
A  M  I  S  S  I  O  N  C  T  Y  T  H  U
O  C  O  N  T  A  C  T  S  G  Y  U  X  B
G  H  U  M  A  N  I  T  Y  Q  H  O  E  L
C  O  M  M  U  N  I  T  Y  Q  Y  Y  K  I
L  G  J  W  X  H  O  N  E  S  T  Y  P  C
```

CHARITY	HISTORY
COMMUNITY	HONESTY
CONTACTS	HUMANITY
DONATE	YOUTH
FINANCE	GOALS
FUNDS	MISSION
GENEROSITY	NEED
PEOPLE	CHILDREN
GLOBAL	PROGRAMS
GROUPS	PUBLIC

85 - Comida #2

```
C Y C G P P U B N I W G C S
H R E I V M I R A O Z A H U
E A L N W J I G G S R Y O N
R R E G K I T A R M F Q C F
R T R E N E K C I H C V O L
Y I Y R Z L C H E E S E L O
Q C D F R P G N G M Y D A W
Y H C R P P E C M C A P T E
O O T V Q A O T A M O T E R
G K T T X K F O N B F Z L H
U E P A R G W C A L M O N D
R B L E L W G G N D E C I R
T Z E H M W T N A L P G G E
T F S W D A E R B H G T G F
```

ARTICHOKE	KIWI
ALMOND	APPLE
CELERY	BREAD
RICE	BANANA
EGGPLANT	CHICKEN
CHERRY	CHEESE
CHOCOLATE	TOMATO
SUNFLOWER	WHEAT
EGG	GRAPE
GINGER	YOGURT

86 - Arte

```
C Y G K Q O Y P F U E J B H
H E P T D U Q O S I E E P P
E O R E O J A R Y S G R J E
X C N A O Y B T M U V U R X
P O P E M B J R B R I T R Z
R M A C S I K A O R S P Z E
E P I C T T C Y L E U L P L
S O N O I C O R B A A U H P
S S T M K E A T W L L C X M
I I I P N J D E R I P S N I
O T N L Q B A O T S P E V S
N I G E W U Y P G M U I N N
J O S X F S O R I G I N A L
A N C R E A T E W P E E Z L
```

CERAMIC   ORIGINAL
COMPLEX   PAINTINGS
COMPOSITION   POETRY
CREATE   PORTRAY
SCULPTURE   SIMPLE
EXPRESSION   SYMBOL
FIGURE   SURREALISM
HONEST   SUBJECT
MOOD   VISUAL
INSPIRED

87 - Diplomacia

```
C D I S C U S S I O N H B N
N O I T U L O S E R Z M E Q
T P N O I T A R E P O O C E
K I R F J U S T I C E C U T
G H K F L A D V I S E R O H
S O X Y T I N U M M O C T I
O E V K O S C I T I L O P C
L M B E A E F T A A Y E G S
U B G H R O D A S S A B M A
T A X M O N S E C U R I T Y
I S C I T A M O L P I D K I
O S G N N G I E R O F N N Y
N Y T I R G E T N I P N F P
L A N G U A G E S T Q F Z U
```

ADVISER	ETHICS
COMMUNITY	GOVERNMENT
CONFLICT	LANGUAGES
COOPERATION	INTEGRITY
DIPLOMATIC	JUSTICE
DISCUSSION	POLITICS
EMBASSY	RESOLUTION
AMBASSADOR	SECURITY
FOREIGN	SOLUTION

88 - Herboristería

```
O G B C P P S Y T I L A U Q
U A D R O V A L F N C P T Q
Z R L I G H F P U G U A A K
Q D H K L K F F T R L R R D
C E Y L E L R O Z E I S R H
L N R P N D O Y Q D N L A F
A K X D N H N H Q I A E G G
V R O S E M A R Y E R Y O A
E Z Z X F G D G K N Y N N H
N G A R L I C K Z T N A L P
D G R E E N F V W N Q F I Q
E A R O M A T I C I G D S A
R E W O L F U T D M E Q A Q
Y M A R J O R A M W C A B P
```

GARLIC
BASIL
AROMATIC
SAFFRON
QUALITY
CULINARY
DILL
TARRAGON
FLOWER
FENNEL

INGREDIENT
GARDEN
LAVENDER
MARJORAM
MINT
PARSLEY
PLANT
ROSEMARY
FLAVOR
GREEN

89 - Energía

```
S  K  E  E  F  E  O  F  D  T  G  N  O  R
T  T  D  L  Q  L  W  D  I  Y  A  U  P  E
F  U  E  H  E  M  T  H  E  I  S  C  W  N
E  U  N  A  M  C  A  U  S  M  O  L  S  E
L  P  E  A  M  R  T  A  E  H  L  E  U  W
E  Y  G  L  D  J  Y  R  L  N  I  A  N  A
C  N  O  T  O  H  P  O  O  P  N  R  X  B
T  G  R  Z  Z  F  O  T  W  N  E  W  R  L
R  C  D  N  I  W  R  O  I  O  V  M  A  E
I  I  Y  U  L  J  T  M  D  B  M  D  I  I
C  B  H  A  S  B  N  D  O  R  I  C  I  L
T  U  R  B  I  N  E  K  E  A  W  O  W  W
P  O  L  L  U  T  I  O  N  C  U  Y  Z  R
I  N  D  U  S  T  R  Y  R  E  T  T  A  B
```

BATTERY	GASOLINE
HEAT	HYDROGEN
CARBON	INDUSTRY
FUEL	MOTOR
POLLUTION	NUCLEAR
DIESEL	RENEWABLE
ELECTRON	SUN
ELECTRIC	TURBINE
ENTROPY	STEAM
PHOTON	WIND

90 - Insectos

```
B D S L M W Q C P I H Y L M
U R A A O A S I T N A M A O
T A H D T S J C A W K E R S
T G M Y H P L A E P W E V Q
E O H B B W S D L Y H T A U
R N L U R E O A F Q C I A I
F F Z G X E E R K L A M D T
L L Z X G B M T M A O R O O
Y Y Y B K Q U E L H R E K M
R V E U H G T N M E K T W I
K Q P H V S Z R R H C K G N
S K W T S U C O L C O M Y Z
J J G A F A I H Z O C A N T
G R A S S H O P P E R H Q E
```

BEE	LARVA
WASP	DRAGONFLY
HORNET	MANTIS
APHID	BUTTERFLY
CICADA	LADYBUG
COCKROACH	MOSQUITO
BEETLE	MOTH
WORM	FLEA
ANT	GRASSHOPPER
LOCUST	TERMITE

91 - Especias

```
P G L P M G Y N V F Q Q K N
C A V A N I L L A P K V Z B
U U P N U T M E G E A S M I
M B Y R R U C J X C N W C T
I J W C I L R A G I I E O T
N O D F J K L V S R S E N E
P E P P E R A F A O E T I R
C I N N A M O N L C P X O F
W T D Z L R G A T I P W N L
S A F F R O N I C L O V E A
M I U U Q V L E N N E F V V
S C A Q M Z O D F G K H F O
V L B O H S O U R Z E H R R
E J Y N B L D P F E T R H A
```

SOUR	SWEET
GARLIC	FENNEL
BITTER	GINGER
ANISE	NUTMEG
SAFFRON	PAPRIKA
CINNAMON	PEPPER
ONION	LICORICE
CLOVE	FLAVOR
CUMIN	SALT
CURRY	VANILLA

92 - Emociones

```
T  E  N  D  E  R  N  E  S  S  S  R  C  F
F  V  R  I  P  Y  N  V  H  R  Y  E  P  Q
G  O  B  O  R  E  D  O  M  H  M  L  A  C
H  L  U  F  E  T  A  R  G  M  P  A  W  F
L  Q  K  I  G  M  N  L  A  C  A  X  F  E
X  J  M  J  N  C  R  E  R  K  T  E  E  I
I  I  L  C  A  L  L  B  T  I  H  D  A  J
S  A  T  I  S  F  I  E  D  N  Y  R  R  O
R  E  L  I  E  F  P  X  L  D  O  V  Z  Y
S  U  R  P  R  I  S  E  O  N  U  C  N  X
B  L  I  S  S  H  F  U  X  E  C  A  E  P
S  A  D  N  E  S  S  O  V  S  I  K  L  Q
V  B  O  K  H  Y  M  M  K  S  N  G  J  X
E  M  B  A  R  R  A  S  S  E  D  I  R  Z
```

BOREDOM	ANGER
GRATEFUL	FEAR
JOY	PEACE
RELIEF	RELAXED
LOVE	SATISFIED
EMBARRASSED	SYMPATHY
BLISS	SURPRISE
KINDNESS	TENDERNESS
CALM	SADNESS
CONTENT	

93 - Jazz

```
Y G F E O C M K R Z K P L N
G B E L E O U Z J Q Y J V E
W C Y N O L S I S A H P M E
S A L G R D I X A L Q A R M
E M W X E E C Z A E Z Z W C
I M P R O V I S A T I O N M
A L B U M T A L E N T I N V
F A M O U S S C O N C E R T
S A V D E U Q I N H C E T R
M T S O N G B Q T H S U Z H
U E Y O H Y B C T R J L Z Y
R S X L Y P O W I G A I N T
D K F S E T I R O V A F E H
C O M P O S I T I O N F W M
```

ARTIST
ALBUM
SONG
COMPOSITION
CONCERT
STYLE
EMPHASIS
FAMOUS
FAVORITES

GENRE
IMPROVISATION
MUSIC
NEW
RHYTHM
TALENT
DRUMS
TECHNIQUE
OLD

94 - Mediciones

```
L E N G T H M M E T E R Q Z
Y T O J H G A K S K U R K G
U Y T O G L S A C E U S F D
Z B P W I R S C A M U R E F
B X R E E W M I N U T E E H
A O Y M W E W C E L U T K D
D E G R E E I A G O Z I T E
I N C H J O D U R V W L J C
T X W C L N T H E I G H T I
D L G E Z U H Y F S S C C M
V E U R E T E M I T N E C A
B M P D A K I L O G R A M L
X R E T E M O L I K A V C G
W F H A H O U N C E F J I Q
```

HEIGHT	LENGTH
WIDTH	MASS
BYTE	METER
CENTIMETER	MINUTE
DECIMAL	OUNCE
DEGREE	WEIGHT
GRAM	DEPTH
KILOGRAM	INCH
KILOMETER	TON
LITER	VOLUME

95 - Barcos

```
B  E  Q  Z  U  X  V  A  G  T  N  N  E  E
U  D  A  A  S  J  H  I  N  M  A  O  M  Q
O  K  B  U  N  C  E  J  A  C  T  A  I  H
Y  S  Y  S  W  R  I  P  E  O  H  E  T  K
U  D  A  L  R  E  M  Z  C  K  C  O  I  E
B  D  F  I  F  W  A  S  O  L  A  N  R  M
T  U  A  C  L  X  S  A  Z  B  Y  A  A  G
F  E  R  R  Y  O  T  I  H  J  E  C  M  D
A  K  E  G  T  V  R  L  K  A  Y  A  K  A
R  A  V  F  H  U  K  B  B  X  J  G  I  Z
B  L  I  N  R  T  A  O  B  F  T  M  K  Z
Y  E  R  T  O  C  L  A  C  I  T  U  A  N
T  I  D  E  P  Y  M  T  E  N  G  I  N  E
P  U  P  V  E  X  P  V  A  S  K  W  Z  T
```

ANCHOR	SAILOR
RAFT	MARITIME
BUOY	MAST
CANOE	ENGINE
ROPE	NAUTICAL
FERRY	OCEAN
KAYAK	RIVER
LAKE	CREW
SEA	SAILBOAT
TIDE	YACHT

96 - Antártida

```
C V X W P K M Q G R F C K C
T O P B A V L M L O O O P U
T E N I P T U V A C P N E P
B S M S Y U E I C K K T N S
V D K P E Q W R I Y N I G R
T N D W E X C E I B N U E
D A T L Q R V K R C I E I S
G L J T D X A A S E R N N E
F S V A P J R T T E D T S A
M I N E R A L S U I S Z Y R
C L O U D S Z F V R O T R C
S C I E N T I F I C E N X H
E X P E D I T I O N C S W E
W C G E O G R A P H Y A B R
```

WATER   RESEARCHER
BAY   ISLANDS
SCIENTIFIC   MINERALS
CONSERVATION   CLOUDS
CONTINENT   BIRDS
EXPEDITION   PENGUINS
GEOGRAPHY   ROCKY
GLACIERS   TEMPERATURE
ICE

97 - Mamíferos

```
S M R S J U O V D K K B O H
B D U X H D Z O O R A E B O
C A M E L E O V L N N M H R
C Q W Q C R E G P J G M F S
Y X O F O A A P H D A R G E
B V L H Y B X F I A R B E Z
G U F X O B C O N G O G K I
K H L L T I X P N I O C Y W
L X Z L E T R H D R K A K H
V M O N K E Y R O A L T R A
E L E P H A N T N F V V V L
G O R I L L A R K F P N W E
S U K M Y L R L E E E N O P
A R J M S G X M Y A O L U Y
```

WHALE	CAT
DONKEY	GORILLA
HORSE	GIRAFFE
CAMEL	WOLF
KANGAROO	MONKEY
ZEBRA	BEAR
RABBIT	SHEEP
COYOTE	DOG
DOLPHIN	BULL
ELEPHANT	FOX

98 - Boxeo

```
O N B M Q X E L L E B R R S
P P S E V O L G Y X Y O E W
C I P K C I K C S H K P F S
K Q Q O I X K H T A J E E Y
C Z J P N L R I R U O S R S
I S E Z H E L N E S F I E V
U N N N O I N S N T I D E E
Q F J F I S T T G E G B H A
V Z H U B C T N T D H O X F
Y C R C R O X I H I T D Z H
E L B O W I K O F A E Y M G
C O R N E R E P P D R X V Z
B V I G P I Y S U C O F C E
W Q Q J V S R E C O V E R Y
```

REFEREE	GLOVES
CHIN	SKILL
BELL	INJURIES
FOCUS	FIGHTER
ELBOW	OPPONENT
ROPES	KICK
BODY	POINTS
CORNER	FIST
EXHAUSTED	QUICK
STRENGTH	RECOVERY

99 - Abejas

```
Y  H  I  V  E  G  W  E  Z  Y  D  W  G  J
T  I  U  R  F  L  A  N  N  P  F  E  S  Q
I  A  E  A  B  Y  Q  R  I  L  P  O  G  S
S  W  A  R  M  H  M  K  D  S  U  N  O  K
R  S  C  D  C  W  O  T  U  E  W  A  X  D
E  F  Q  D  R  S  G  N  I  W  N  I  B  S
V  N  W  J  N  T  N  E  E  I  E  N  L  V
I  P  L  A  N  T  S  E  P  Y  L  S  O  Z
D  F  J  F  V  P  D  U  S  Q  L  E  S  K
F  L  O  W  E  R  S  Q  C  R  O  C  S  X
B  E  N  E  F  I  C  I  A  L  P  T  O  R
E  C  O  S  Y  S  T  E  M  C  H  K  M  I
S  M  O  K  E  J  E  C  O  L  E  B  K  L
P  O  L  L  I  N  A  T  O  R  K  O  I  H
```

WINGS	FRUIT
BENEFICIAL	SMOKE
WAX	INSECT
HIVE	GARDEN
FOOD	HONEY
DIVERSITY	PLANTS
ECOSYSTEM	POLLEN
SWARM	POLLINATOR
BLOSSOM	QUEEN
FLOWERS	SUN

100 - Psicología

```
A P P O I N T M E N T T C S
U F X R O I V A H E B H O U
X L L O Y T E S P E I O G B
D L A Y V H M S E P D U N C
S M C Z Y E O E R E E G I O
M E I W R T S C R A H T N
L L N E I A I S E S S T I S
R B I S L P O M P O E S O C
V O L C A Y N E T N F G N I
D R C R E T S N I A M L O O
G P N Q R P I T O L D J E U
D R E A M S P O N I V T Z S
C O N F L I C T N T T A A A
C H I L D H O O D Y I F G R
```

APPOINTMENT
CLINICAL
COGNITION
BEHAVIOR
CONFLICT
EGO
EMOTIONS
ASSESSMENT
IDEAS
CHILDHOOD

THOUGHTS
PERCEPTION
PERSONALITY
PROBLEM
REALITY
SENSATION
SUBCONSCIOUS
DREAMS
THERAPY

1 - Arqueología

2 - Granja #2

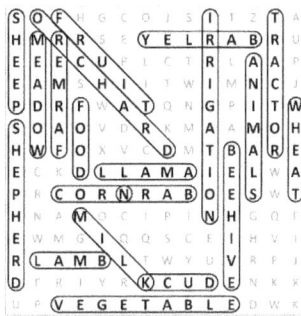

3 - La Empresa

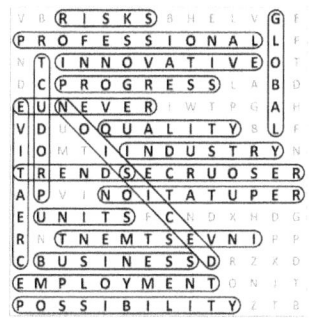

4 - Mueble

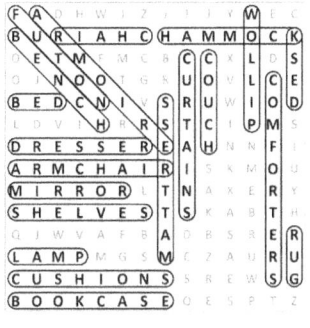

5 - Aviones

6 - Tipos de Cabello

7 - Ética

8 - Ciencia Ficción

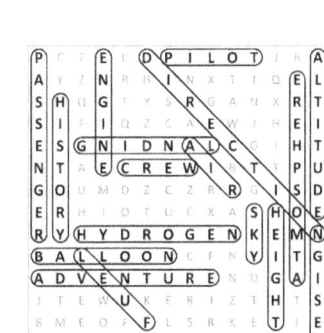

9 - Circo

10 - Granja #1

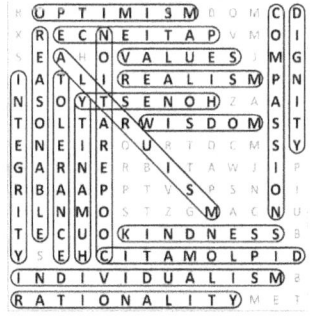

11 - Camping

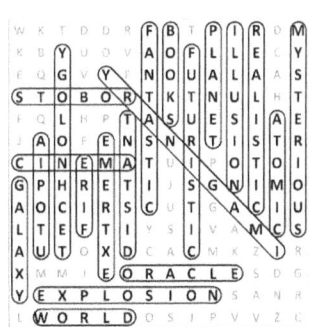

12 - Fruta

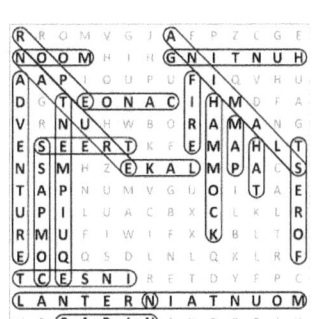

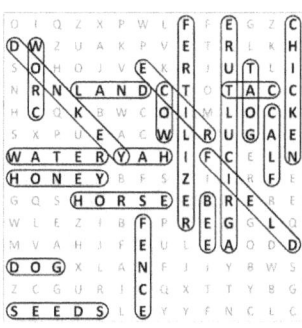

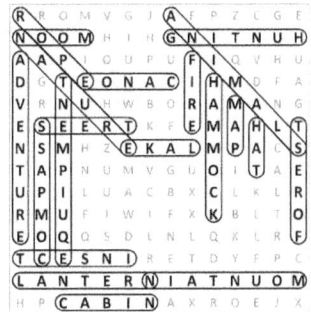

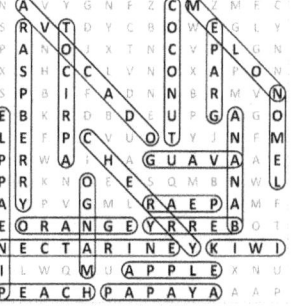

13 - Geología

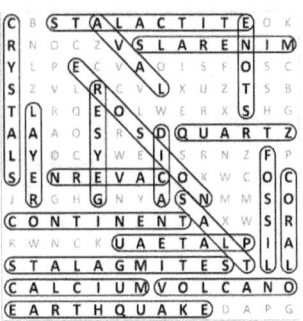

14 - Álgebra

15 - Plantas

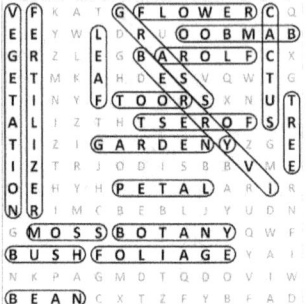

16 - Suministros de Arte

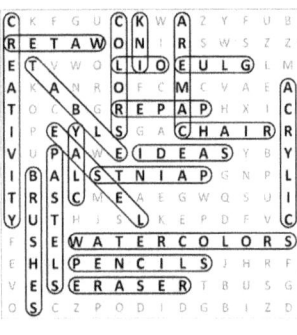

17 - Negocio

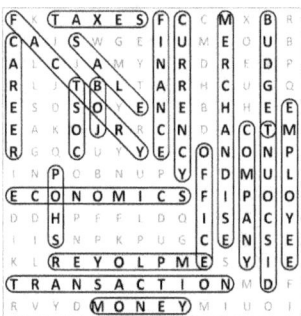

18 - Jardín

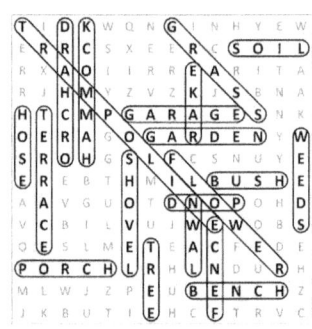

19 - Países #2

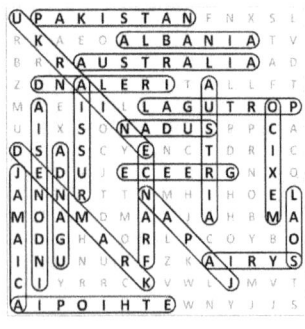

20 - Números

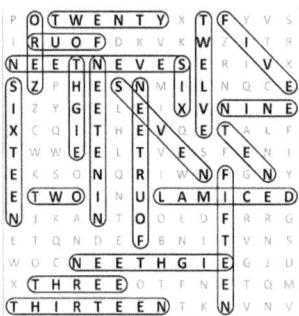

21 - Física

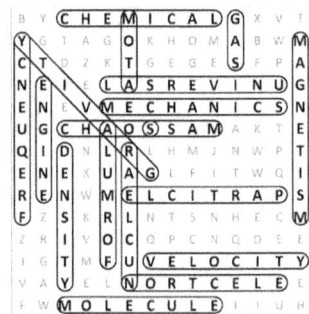

22 - Belleza

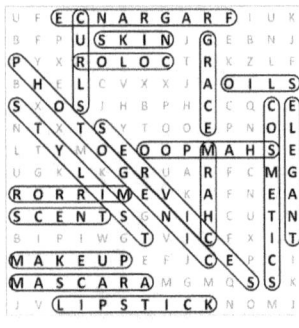

23 - Países #1

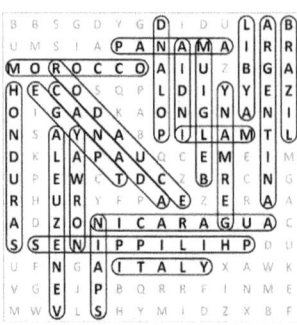

24 - Mitología

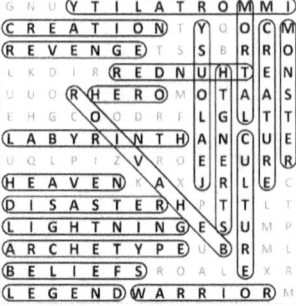

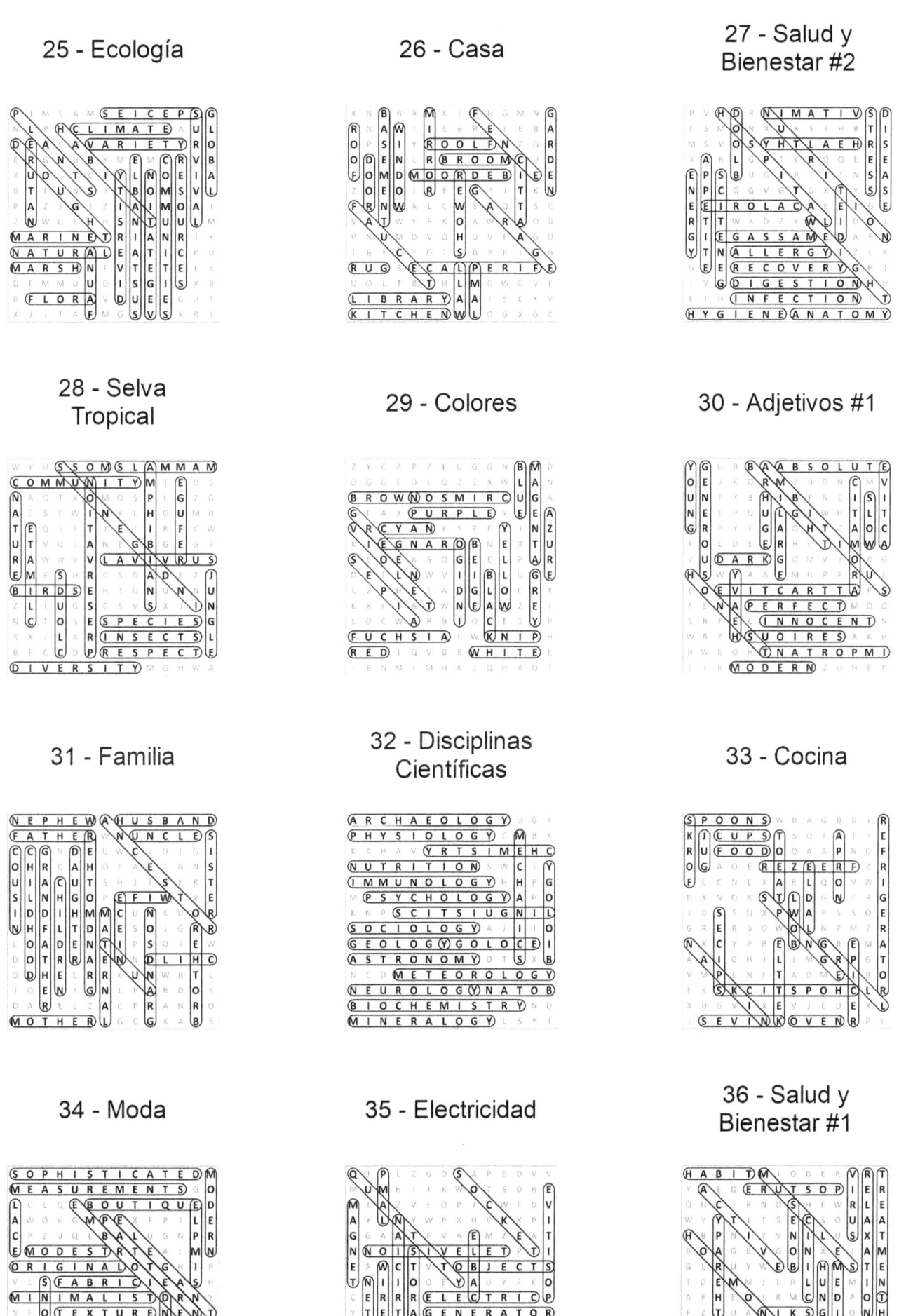

25 - Ecología

26 - Casa

27 - Salud y Bienestar #2

28 - Selva Tropical

29 - Colores

30 - Adjetivos #1

31 - Familia

32 - Disciplinas Científicas

33 - Cocina

34 - Moda

35 - Electricidad

36 - Salud y Bienestar #1

37 - Adjetivos #2

38 - Cuerpo Humano

39 - Ciencia

40 - Restaurante #2

41 - Profesiones #1

42 - Geometría

43 - Baile

44 - Matemáticas

45 - Restaurante #1

46 - Profesiones #2

47 - Senderismo

48 - Naturaleza

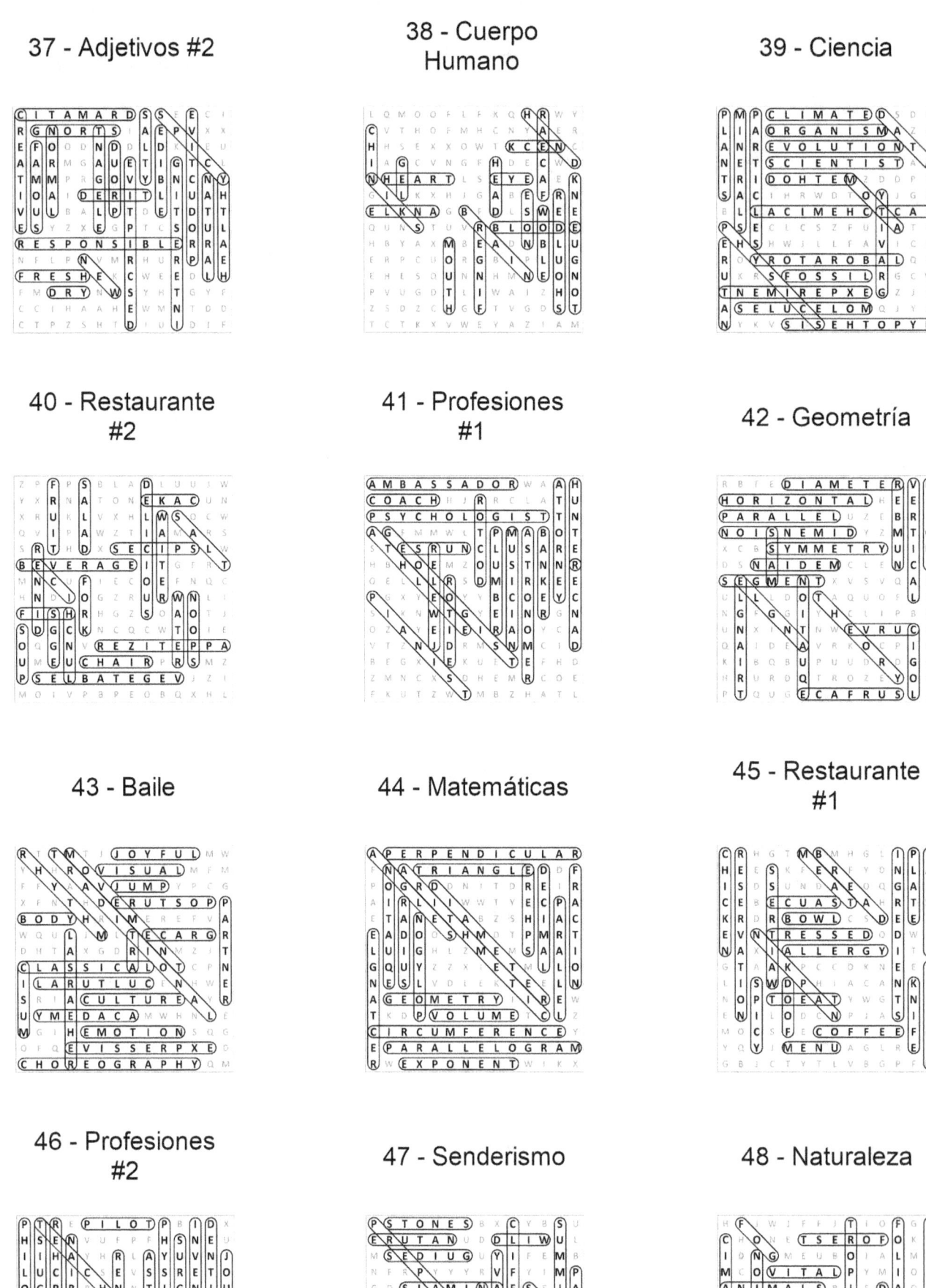

49 - Conduciendo

50 - Ballet

51 - Fuerza y Gravedad

52 - Aventura

53 - Pájaros

54 - Geografía

55 - Música

56 - Actividades

57 - Instrumentos Musicales

58 - Mascotas

59 - Formas

60 - Flores

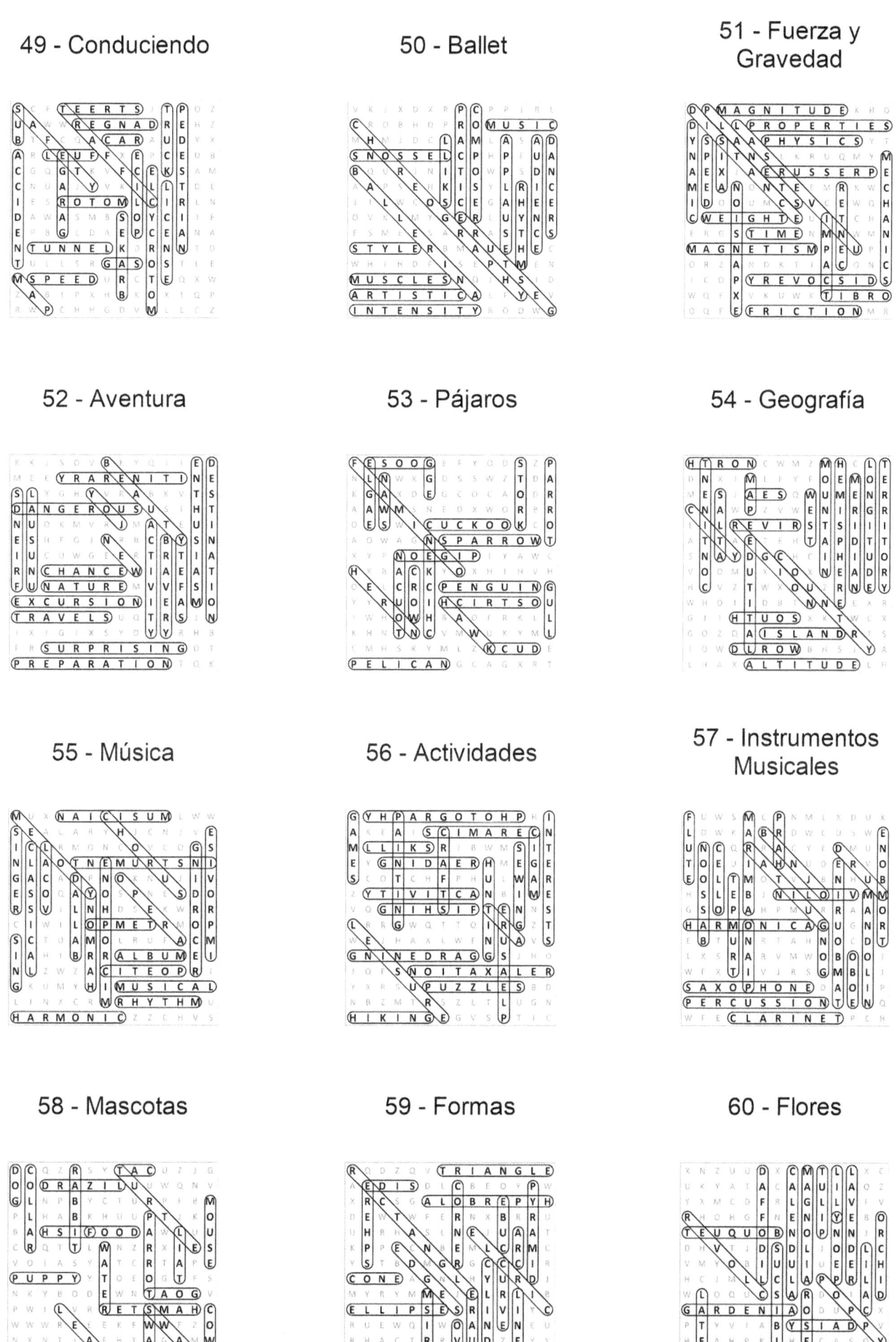

61 - Astronomía

62 - Paisajes

63 - Días y Meses

64 - Jardinería

65 - Chocolate

66 - Barbacoas

67 - Ropa

68 - Meditación

69 - Café

70 - Libros

71 - Los Medios de Comunicación

72 - Nutrición

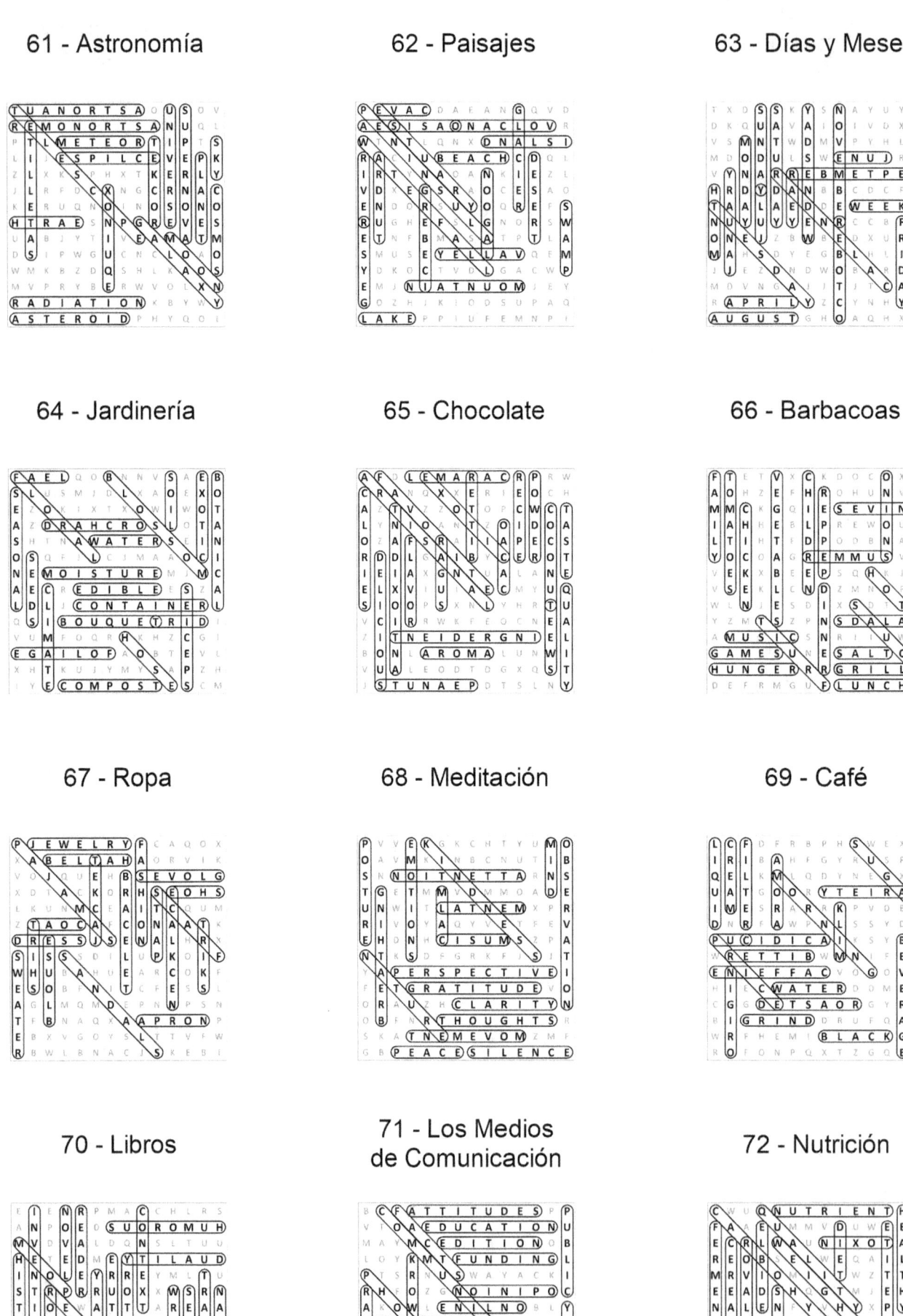

73 - Edificios

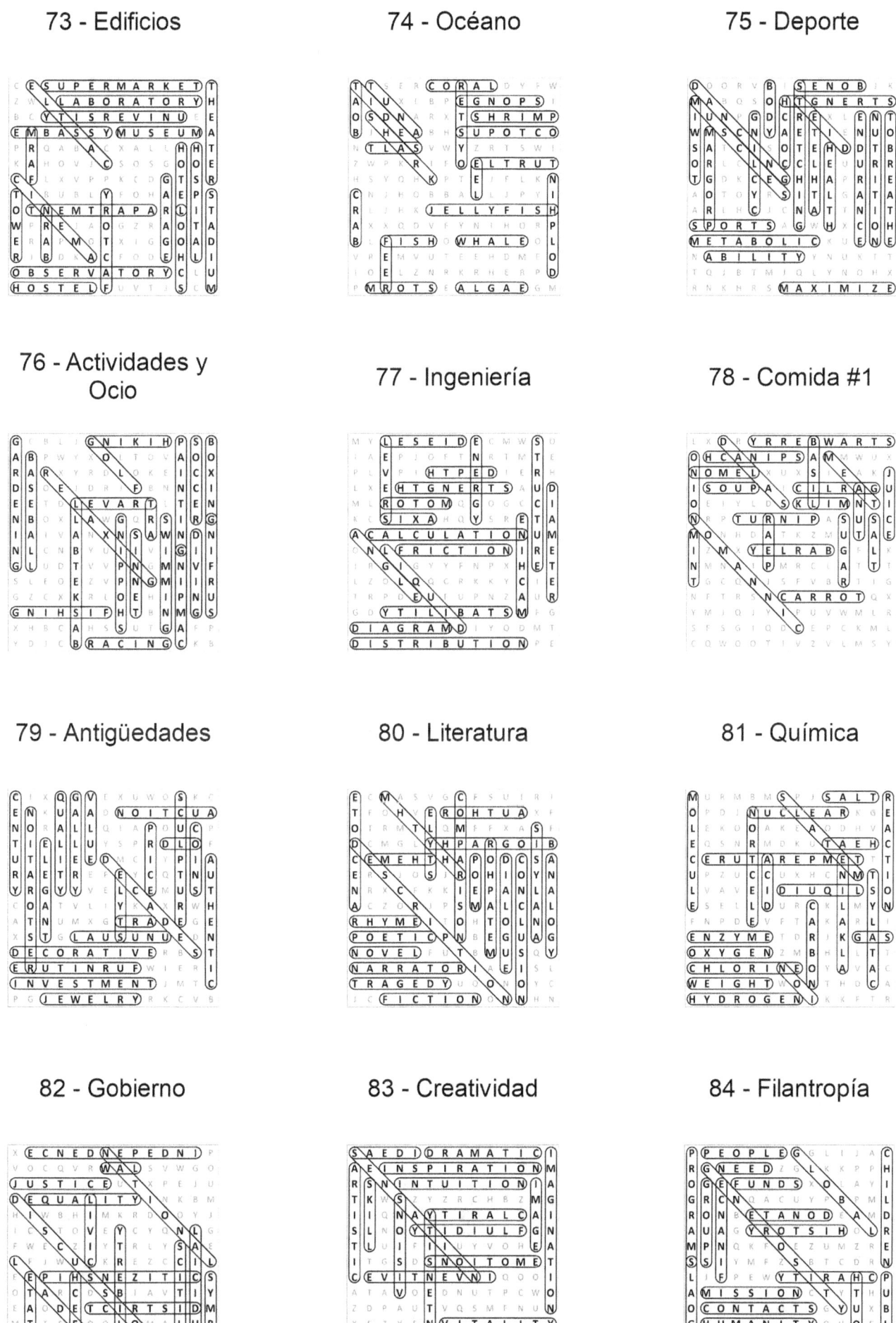

74 - Océano

75 - Deporte

76 - Actividades y Ocio

77 - Ingeniería

78 - Comida #1

79 - Antigüedades

80 - Literatura

81 - Química

82 - Gobierno

83 - Creatividad

84 - Filantropía

85 - Comida #2

86 - Arte

87 - Diplomacia

88 - Herboristería

89 - Energía

90 - Insectos

91 - Especias

92 - Emociones

93 - Jazz

94 - Mediciones

95 - Barcos

96 - Antártida

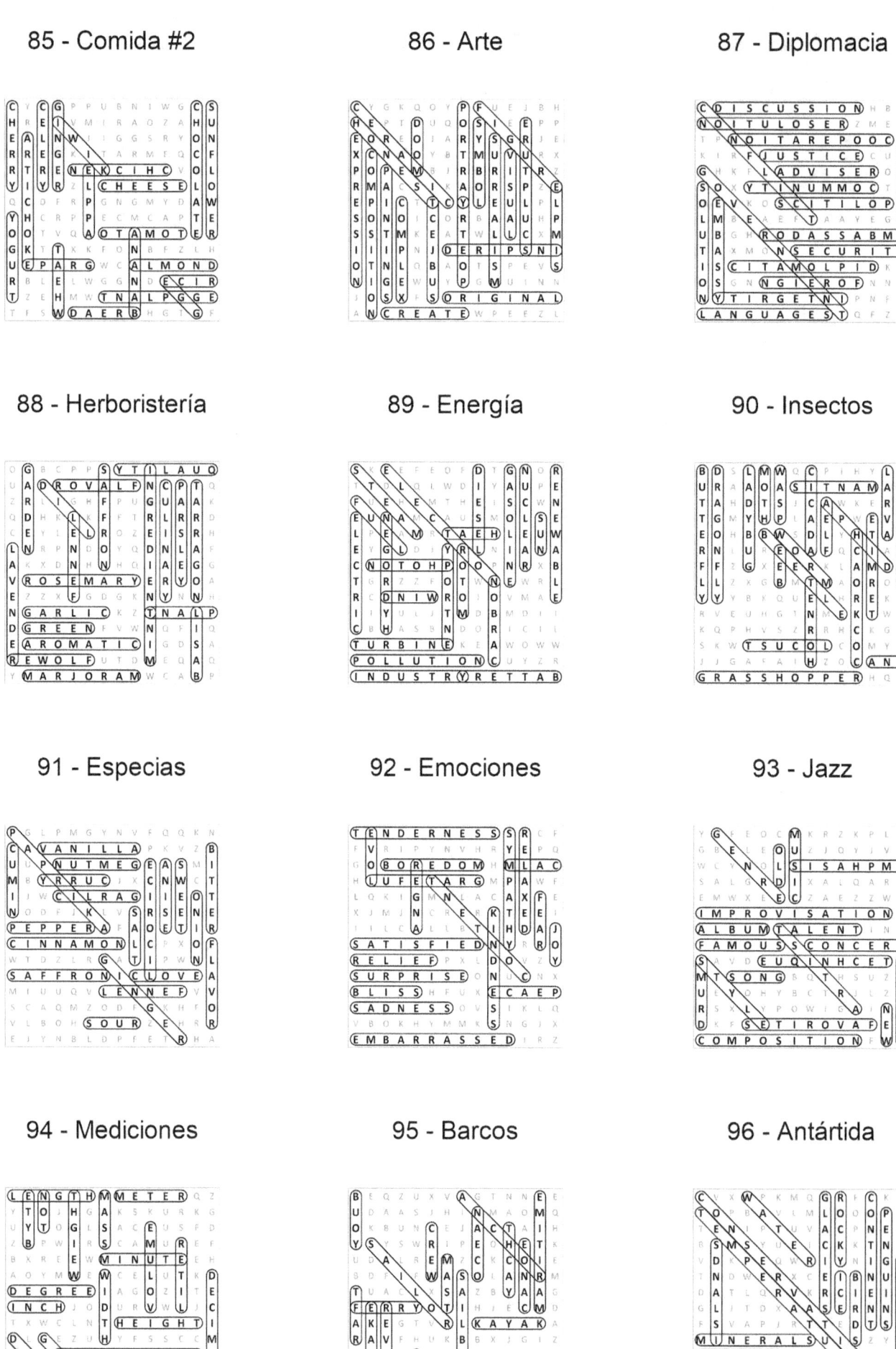

97 - Mamíferos

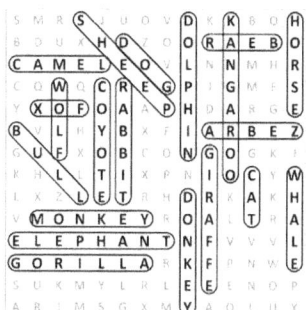

98 - Boxeo

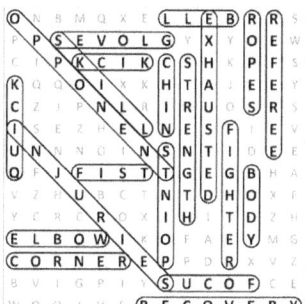

99 - Abejas

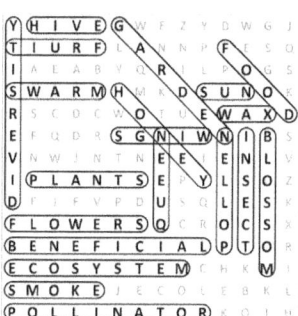

100 - Psicología

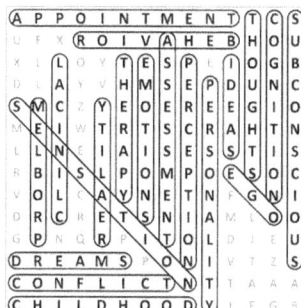

Diccionario

Abejas
Bees

Alas	Wings
Beneficioso	Beneficial
Cera	Wax
Colmena	Hive
Comida	Food
Diversidad	Diversity
Ecosistema	Ecosystem
Enjambre	Swarm
Flor	Blossom
Flores	Flowers
Fruta	Fruit
Humo	Smoke
Insecto	Insect
Jardín	Garden
Miel	Honey
Plantas	Plants
Polen	Pollen
Polinizador	Pollinator
Reina	Queen
Sol	Sun

Actividades
Activities

Actividad	Activity
Arte	Art
Artesanía	Crafts
Caza	Hunting
Cerámica	Ceramics
Costura	Sewing
Fotografía	Photography
Habilidad	Skill
Intereses	Interests
Jardinería	Gardening
Juegos	Games
Lectura	Reading
Magia	Magic
Ocio	Leisure
Pesca	Fishing
Pintura	Painting
Placer	Pleasure
Relajación	Relaxation
Rompecabezas	Puzzles
Senderismo	Hiking

Actividades y Ocio
Activities and Leisure

Arte	Art
Baloncesto	Basketball
Béisbol	Baseball
Boxeo	Boxing
Buceo	Diving
Camping	Camping
Carreras	Racing
Compras	Shopping
Fútbol	Soccer
Golf	Golf
Jardinería	Gardening
Natación	Swimming
Pesca	Fishing
Pintura	Painting
Relajante	Relaxing
Senderismo	Hiking
Surf	Surfing
Tenis	Tennis
Viaje	Travel
Voleibol	Volleyball

Adjetivos #1
Adjectives #1

Absoluto	Absolute
Activo	Active
Ambicioso	Ambitious
Aromático	Aromatic
Atractivo	Attractive
Brillante	Bright
Enorme	Huge
Generoso	Generous
Grande	Large
Honesto	Honest
Importante	Important
Inocente	Innocent
Joven	Young
Lento	Slow
Moderno	Modern
Oscuro	Dark
Perfecto	Perfect
Pesado	Heavy
Serio	Serious
Valioso	Valuable

Adjetivos #2
Adjectives #2

Cansado	Tired
Comestible	Edible
Creativo	Creative
Descriptivo	Descriptive
Dramático	Dramatic
Elegante	Elegant
Famoso	Famous
Fresco	Fresh
Fuerte	Strong
Interesante	Interesting
Natural	Natural
Normal	Normal
Nuevo	New
Orgulloso	Proud
Picante	Spicy
Productivo	Productive
Responsable	Responsible
Salado	Salty
Saludable	Healthy
Seco	Dry

Antártida
Antarctica

Agua	Water
Bahía	Bay
Científico	Scientific
Conservación	Conservation
Continente	Continent
Expedición	Expedition
Geografía	Geography
Glaciares	Glaciers
Hielo	Ice
Investigador	Researcher
Islas	Islands
Migración	Migration
Minerales	Minerals
Nubes	Clouds
Pájaros	Birds
Península	Peninsula
Pingüinos	Penguins
Rocoso	Rocky
Temperatura	Temperature
Topografía	Topography

Antigüedades
Antiques

Arte	Art
Auténtico	Authentic
Calidad	Quality
Decorativo	Decorative
Décadas	Decades
Elegante	Elegant
Escultura	Sculpture
Estilo	Style
Galería	Gallery
Inusual	Unusual
Inversión	Investment
Joyas	Jewelry
Monedas	Coins
Mueble	Furniture
Precio	Price
Restauración	Restoration
Siglo	Century
Subasta	Auction
Valor	Value
Viejo	Old

Arqueología
Archeology

Análisis	Analysis
Antigüedad	Antiquity
Años	Years
Civilización	Civilization
Descendiente	Descendant
Desconocido	Unknown
Equipo	Team
Era	Era
Evaluación	Evaluation
Experto	Expert
Fósil	Fossil
Huesos	Bones
Investigador	Researcher
Misterio	Mystery
Objetos	Objects
Olvidado	Forgotten
Profesor	Professor
Reliquia	Relic
Templo	Temple
Tumba	Tomb

Arte
Art

Cerámica	Ceramic
Complejo	Complex
Composición	Composition
Crear	Create
Escultura	Sculpture
Expresión	Expression
Figura	Figure
Honesto	Honest
Humor	Mood
Inspirado	Inspired
Original	Original
Personal	Personal
Pinturas	Paintings
Poesía	Poetry
Retratar	Portray
Sencillo	Simple
Símbolo	Symbol
Surrealismo	Surrealism
Tema	Subject
Visual	Visual

Astronomía
Astronomy

Asteroide	Asteroid
Astronauta	Astronaut
Astrónomo	Astronomer
Cielo	Sky
Cohete	Rocket
Constelación	Constellation
Cosmos	Cosmos
Eclipse	Eclipse
Equinoccio	Equinox
Galaxia	Galaxy
Luna	Moon
Meteoro	Meteor
Observatorio	Observatory
Planeta	Planet
Radiación	Radiation
Satélite	Satellite
Supernova	Supernova
Telescopio	Telescope
Tierra	Earth
Universo	Universe

Aventura
Adventure

Actividad	Activity
Alegría	Joy
Amigos	Friends
Belleza	Beauty
Destino	Destination
Dificultad	Difficulty
Entusiasmo	Enthusiasm
Excursión	Excursion
Inusual	Unusual
Itinerario	Itinerary
Naturaleza	Nature
Navegación	Navigation
Nuevo	New
Oportunidad	Chance
Peligroso	Dangerous
Preparación	Preparation
Seguridad	Safety
Sorprendente	Surprising
Valentía	Bravery
Viajes	Travels

Aviones
Airplanes

Aire	Air
Altitud	Altitude
Altura	Height
Aterrizaje	Landing
Atmósfera	Atmosphere
Aventura	Adventure
Cielo	Sky
Combustible	Fuel
Construcción	Construction
Dirección	Direction
Diseño	Design
Globo	Balloon
Hélices	Propellers
Hidrógeno	Hydrogen
Historia	History
Motor	Engine
Pasajero	Passenger
Piloto	Pilot
Tripulación	Crew
Turbulencia	Turbulence

Álgebra
Algebra

Cantidad	Quantity
Cero	Zero
Diagrama	Diagram
División	Division
Ecuación	Equation
Exponente	Exponent
Factor	Factor
Falso	False
Fórmula	Formula
Fracción	Fraction
Infinito	Infinite
Lineal	Linear
Matriz	Matrix
Número	Number
Paréntesis	Parenthesis
Problema	Problem
Resta	Subtraction
Simplificar	Simplify
Solución	Solution
Variable	Variable

Baile
Dance

Academia	Academy
Alegre	Joyful
Arte	Art
Clásico	Classical
Coreografía	Choreography
Cuerpo	Body
Cultura	Culture
Cultural	Cultural
Emoción	Emotion
Ensayo	Rehearsal
Expresivo	Expressive
Gracia	Grace
Movimiento	Movement
Música	Music
Postura	Posture
Ritmo	Rhythm
Saltar	Jump
Socio	Partner
Tradicional	Traditional
Visual	Visual

Ballet
Ballet

Aplauso	Applause
Artístico	Artistic
Audiencia	Audience
Bailarina	Ballerina
Bailarines	Dancers
Compositor	Composer
Coreografía	Choreography
Ensayo	Rehearsal
Estilo	Style
Expresivo	Expressive
Gesto	Gesture
Habilidad	Skill
Intensidad	Intensity
Lecciones	Lessons
Músculos	Muscles
Música	Music
Orquesta	Orchestra
Práctica	Practice
Ritmo	Rhythm
Técnica	Technique

Barbacoas
Barbecues

Almuerzo	Lunch
Caliente	Hot
Cebollas	Onions
Cena	Dinner
Cuchillos	Knives
Ensaladas	Salads
Familia	Family
Fruta	Fruit
Hambre	Hunger
Juegos	Games
Música	Music
Niños	Children
Parrilla	Grill
Pimienta	Pepper
Pollo	Chicken
Sal	Salt
Salsa	Sauce
Tomates	Tomatoes
Verano	Summer
Verduras	Vegetables

Barcos
Boats

Ancla	Anchor
Balsa	Raft
Boya	Buoy
Canoa	Canoe
Cuerda	Rope
Ferry	Ferry
Kayak	Kayak
Lago	Lake
Mar	Sea
Marea	Tide
Marinero	Sailor
Marítimo	Maritime
Mástil	Mast
Motor	Engine
Náutico	Nautical
Océano	Ocean
Río	River
Tripulación	Crew
Velero	Sailboat
Yate	Yacht

Belleza
Beauty

Aceites	Oils
Aroma	Scent
Champú	Shampoo
Color	Color
Cosméticos	Cosmetics
Elegancia	Elegance
Elegante	Elegant
Encanto	Charm
Espejo	Mirror
Estilista	Stylist
Fotogénico	Photogenic
Fragancia	Fragrance
Gracia	Grace
Maquillaje	Makeup
Piel	Skin
Pintalabios	Lipstick
Rizos	Curls
Rímel	Mascara
Servicios	Services
Tijeras	Scissors

Boxeo
Boxing

Árbitro	Referee
Barbilla	Chin
Campana	Bell
Centrar	Focus
Codo	Elbow
Cuerdas	Ropes
Cuerpo	Body
Esquina	Corner
Exhausto	Exhausted
Fuerza	Strength
Guantes	Gloves
Habilidad	Skill
Lesiones	Injuries
Luchador	Fighter
Oponente	Opponent
Patear	Kick
Puntos	Points
Puño	Fist
Rápido	Quick
Recuperación	Recovery

Café
Coffee

Agua	Water
Amargo	Bitter
Aroma	Aroma
Asado	Roasted
Azúcar	Sugar
Ácido	Acidic
Bebida	Beverage
Cafeína	Caffeine
Crema	Cream
Filtro	Filter
Leche	Milk
Líquido	Liquid
Mañana	Morning
Moler	Grind
Negro	Black
Origen	Origin
Precio	Price
Sabor	Flavor
Taza	Cup
Variedad	Variety

Camping
Camping

Animales	Animals
Aventura	Adventure
Árboles	Trees
Bosque	Forest
Brújula	Compass
Cabina	Cabin
Canoa	Canoe
Caza	Hunting
Cuerda	Rope
Equipo	Equipment
Fuego	Fire
Hamaca	Hammock
Insecto	Insect
Lago	Lake
Linterna	Lantern
Luna	Moon
Mapa	Map
Montaña	Mountain
Naturaleza	Nature
Sombrero	Hat

Casa
House

Alfombra	Rug
Ático	Attic
Biblioteca	Library
Chimenea	Fireplace
Cocina	Kitchen
Dormitorio	Bedroom
Ducha	Shower
Escoba	Broom
Espejo	Mirror
Garaje	Garage
Grifo	Faucet
Jardín	Garden
Lámpara	Lamp
Pared	Wall
Piso	Floor
Puerta	Door
Sótano	Basement
Techo	Roof
Valla	Fence
Ventana	Window

Chocolate
Chocolate

Amargo	Bitter
Antioxidante	Antioxidant
Aroma	Aroma
Artesanal	Artisanal
Azúcar	Sugar
Cacahuetes	Peanuts
Cacao	Cacao
Calidad	Quality
Calorías	Calories
Caramelo	Caramel
Coco	Coconut
Delicioso	Delicious
Dulce	Sweet
Exótico	Exotic
Favorito	Favorite
Gusto	Taste
Ingrediente	Ingredient
Polvo	Powder
Receta	Recipe
Sabor	Flavor

Ciencia
Science

Átomo	Atom
Científico	Scientist
Clima	Climate
Datos	Data
Evolución	Evolution
Experimento	Experiment
Física	Physics
Fósil	Fossil
Gravedad	Gravity
Hecho	Fact
Hipótesis	Hypothesis
Laboratorio	Laboratory
Método	Method
Minerales	Minerals
Moléculas	Molecules
Naturaleza	Nature
Organismo	Organism
Partículas	Particles
Plantas	Plants
Químico	Chemical

Ciencia Ficción
Science Fiction

Atómico	Atomic
Cine	Cinema
Distante	Distant
Explosión	Explosion
Extremo	Extreme
Fantástico	Fantastic
Fuego	Fire
Futurista	Futuristic
Galaxia	Galaxy
Ilusión	Illusion
Imaginario	Imaginary
Libros	Books
Misterioso	Mysterious
Mundo	World
Oráculo	Oracle
Planeta	Planet
Realista	Realistic
Robots	Robots
Tecnología	Technology
Utopía	Utopia

Circo
Circus

Acróbata	Acrobat
Animales	Animals
Caramelo	Candy
Carpa	Tent
Desfile	Parade
Elefante	Elephant
Entretener	Entertain
Espectador	Spectator
Globos	Balloons
León	Lion
Magia	Magic
Mago	Magician
Malabarista	Juggler
Mono	Monkey
Mostrar	Show
Música	Music
Payaso	Clown
Tigre	Tiger
Traje	Costume
Truco	Trick

Cocina
Kitchen

Caldera	Kettle
Comer	To Eat
Comida	Food
Congelador	Freezer
Cucharas	Spoons
Cucharón	Ladle
Cuchillos	Knives
Delantal	Apron
Especias	Spices
Esponja	Sponge
Horno	Oven
Jarra	Jug
Palillos	Chopsticks
Parrilla	Grill
Receta	Recipe
Refrigerador	Refrigerator
Servilleta	Napkin
Tazas	Cups
Tazón	Bowl
Tenedores	Forks

Colores
Colors

Amarillo	Yellow
Azul	Blue
Azur	Azure
Beige	Beige
Blanco	White
Carmesí	Crimson
Cian	Cyan
Fucsia	Fuchsia
Gris	Grey
Índigo	Indigo
Magenta	Magenta
Marrón	Brown
Naranja	Orange
Negro	Black
Púrpura	Purple
Rojo	Red
Rosa	Pink
Sepia	Sepia
Verde	Green
Violeta	Violet

Comida #1
Food #1

Ajo	Garlic
Albahaca	Basil
Atún	Tuna
Azúcar	Sugar
Canela	Cinnamon
Carne	Meat
Cebada	Barley
Cebolla	Onion
Ensalada	Salad
Espinacas	Spinach
Fresa	Strawberry
Jugo	Juice
Leche	Milk
Limón	Lemon
Menta	Mint
Nabo	Turnip
Pera	Pear
Sal	Salt
Sopa	Soup
Zanahoria	Carrot

Comida #2
Food #2

Alcachofa	Artichoke
Almendra	Almond
Apio	Celery
Arroz	Rice
Berenjena	Eggplant
Cereza	Cherry
Chocolate	Chocolate
Girasol	Sunflower
Huevo	Egg
Jengibre	Ginger
Kiwi	Kiwi
Manzana	Apple
Pan	Bread
Plátano	Banana
Pollo	Chicken
Queso	Cheese
Tomate	Tomato
Trigo	Wheat
Uva	Grape
Yogur	Yogurt

Conduciendo
Driving

Accidente	Accident
Autobús	Bus
Calle	Street
Camión	Truck
Coche	Car
Combustible	Fuel
Frenos	Brakes
Garaje	Garage
Gas	Gas
Licencia	License
Mapa	Map
Motocicleta	Motorcycle
Motor	Motor
Peatonal	Pedestrian
Peligro	Danger
Policía	Police
Seguridad	Safety
Tráfico	Traffic
Túnel	Tunnel
Velocidad	Speed

Creatividad
Creativity

Artístico	Artistic
Autenticidad	Authenticity
Claridad	Clarity
Dramático	Dramatic
Emociones	Emotions
Espontáneo	Spontaneous
Expresión	Expression
Fluidez	Fluidity
Habilidad	Skill
Ideas	Ideas
Imagen	Image
Imaginación	Imagination
Impresión	Impression
Inspiración	Inspiration
Intensidad	Intensity
Intuición	Intuition
Inventivo	Inventive
Sensación	Sensation
Visiones	Visions
Vitalidad	Vitality

Cuerpo Humano
Human Body

Barbilla	Chin
Boca	Mouth
Cabeza	Head
Cara	Face
Cerebro	Brain
Codo	Elbow
Corazón	Heart
Cuello	Neck
Dedo	Finger
Hombro	Shoulder
Lengua	Tongue
Mano	Hand
Nariz	Nose
Ojo	Eye
Oreja	Ear
Piel	Skin
Pierna	Leg
Rodilla	Knee
Sangre	Blood
Tobillo	Ankle

Deporte
Sport

Atleta	Athlete
Baile	Dancing
Capacidad	Ability
Ciclismo	Cycling
Cuerpo	Body
Deportes	Sports
Dieta	Diet
Entrenador	Coach
Estiramiento	Stretching
Fuerza	Strength
Huesos	Bones
Maximizar	Maximize
Metabólico	Metabolic
Músculos	Muscles
Nadar	To Swim
Nutrición	Nutrition
Programa	Program
Resistencia	Endurance
Respirar	To Breathe
Salud	Health

Diplomacia
Diplomacy

Asesor	Adviser
Comunidad	Community
Conflicto	Conflict
Cooperación	Cooperation
Diplomático	Diplomatic
Discusión	Discussion
Embajada	Embassy
Embajador	Ambassador
Extranjero	Foreign
Ética	Ethics
Gobierno	Government
Humanitario	Humanitarian
Idiomas	Languages
Integridad	Integrity
Justicia	Justice
Política	Politics
Resolución	Resolution
Seguridad	Security
Solución	Solution
Tratado	Treaty

Disciplinas Científicas
Scientific Disciplines

Anatomía	Anatomy
Arqueología	Archaeology
Astronomía	Astronomy
Biología	Biology
Bioquímica	Biochemistry
Botánica	Botany
Ecología	Ecology
Fisiología	Physiology
Geología	Geology
Inmunología	Immunology
Lingüística	Linguistics
Mecánica	Mechanics
Meteorología	Meteorology
Mineralogía	Mineralogy
Neurología	Neurology
Nutrición	Nutrition
Psicología	Psychology
Química	Chemistry
Sociología	Sociology
Zoología	Zoology

Días y Meses
Days and Months

Abril	April
Agosto	August
Año	Year
Calendario	Calendar
Domingo	Sunday
Enero	January
Febrero	February
Jueves	Thursday
Julio	July
Junio	June
Lunes	Monday
Martes	Tuesday
Mes	Month
Miércoles	Wednesday
Noviembre	November
Octubre	October
Sábado	Saturday
Semana	Week
Septiembre	September
Viernes	Friday

Ecología
Ecology

Clima	Climate
Comunidades	Communities
Diversidad	Diversity
Especie	Species
Fauna	Fauna
Flora	Flora
Global	Global
Hábitat	Habitat
Marino	Marine
Natural	Natural
Naturaleza	Nature
Pantano	Marsh
Plantas	Plants
Recursos	Resources
Sequía	Drought
Sostenible	Sustainable
Supervivencia	Survival
Variedad	Variety
Vegetación	Vegetation
Voluntarios	Volunteers

Edificios
Buildings

Albergue	Hostel
Apartamento	Apartment
Castillo	Castle
Cine	Cinema
Embajada	Embassy
Escuela	School
Estadio	Stadium
Fábrica	Factory
Garaje	Garage
Granero	Barn
Granja	Farm
Hospital	Hospital
Hotel	Hotel
Laboratorio	Laboratory
Museo	Museum
Observatorio	Observatory
Supermercado	Supermarket
Teatro	Theater
Torre	Tower
Universidad	University

Electricidad
Electricity

Almacenamiento	Storage
Batería	Battery
Bombilla	Bulb
Cable	Cable
Cables	Wires
Cantidad	Quantity
Electricista	Electrician
Eléctrico	Electric
Enchufe	Socket
Equipo	Equipment
Generador	Generator
Imán	Magnet
Lámpara	Lamp
Láser	Laser
Negativo	Negative
Objetos	Objects
Positivo	Positive
Red	Network
Televisión	Television
Teléfono	Telephone

Emociones
Emotions

Aburrimiento	Boredom
Agradecido	Grateful
Alegría	Joy
Alivio	Relief
Amor	Love
Avergonzado	Embarrassed
Beatitud	Bliss
Bondad	Kindness
Calma	Calm
Contenido	Content
Ira	Anger
Miedo	Fear
Paz	Peace
Relajado	Relaxed
Satisfecho	Satisfied
Simpatía	Sympathy
Sorpresa	Surprise
Ternura	Tenderness
Tranquilidad	Tranquility
Tristeza	Sadness

Energía
Energy

Batería	Battery
Calor	Heat
Carbono	Carbon
Combustible	Fuel
Contaminación	Pollution
Diesel	Diesel
Electrón	Electron
Eléctrico	Electric
Entropía	Entropy
Fotón	Photon
Gasolina	Gasoline
Hidrógeno	Hydrogen
Industria	Industry
Motor	Motor
Nuclear	Nuclear
Renovable	Renewable
Sol	Sun
Turbina	Turbine
Vapor	Steam
Viento	Wind

Especias
Spices

Agrio	Sour
Ajo	Garlic
Amargo	Bitter
Anís	Anise
Azafrán	Saffron
Canela	Cinnamon
Cebolla	Onion
Clavo	Clove
Comino	Cumin
Curry	Curry
Dulce	Sweet
Hinojo	Fennel
Jengibre	Ginger
Nuez Moscada	Nutmeg
Pimentón	Paprika
Pimienta	Pepper
Regaliz	Licorice
Sabor	Flavor
Sal	Salt
Vainilla	Vanilla

Ética
Ethics

Altruismo	Altruism
Bondad	Kindness
Compasión	Compassion
Cooperación	Cooperation
Dignidad	Dignity
Diplomático	Diplomatic
Filosofía	Philosophy
Honestidad	Honesty
Humanidad	Humanity
Individualismo	Individualism
Integridad	Integrity
Optimismo	Optimism
Paciencia	Patience
Racionalidad	Rationality
Razonable	Reasonable
Realismo	Realism
Respetuoso	Respectful
Sabiduría	Wisdom
Tolerancia	Tolerance
Valores	Values

Familia
Family

Abuela	Grandmother
Abuelo	Grandfather
Antepasado	Ancestor
Esposa	Wife
Hermana	Sister
Hermano	Brother
Hija	Daughter
Infancia	Childhood
Madre	Mother
Marido	Husband
Materno	Maternal
Nieto	Grandson
Niño	Child
Niños	Children
Padre	Father
Primo	Cousin
Sobrina	Niece
Sobrino	Nephew
Tía	Aunt
Tío	Uncle

Filantropía
Philanthropy

Caridad	Charity
Comunidad	Community
Contactos	Contacts
Donar	Donate
Finanzas	Finance
Fondos	Funds
Generosidad	Generosity
Gente	People
Global	Global
Grupos	Groups
Historia	History
Honestidad	Honesty
Humanidad	Humanity
Juventud	Youth
Metas	Goals
Misión	Mission
Necesitar	Need
Niños	Children
Programas	Programs
Público	Public

Física
Physics

Aceleración	Acceleration
Átomo	Atom
Caos	Chaos
Densidad	Density
Electrón	Electron
Fórmula	Formula
Frecuencia	Frequency
Gas	Gas
Gravedad	Gravity
Magnetismo	Magnetism
Masa	Mass
Mecánica	Mechanics
Molécula	Molecule
Motor	Engine
Nuclear	Nuclear
Partícula	Particle
Químico	Chemical
Relatividad	Relativity
Universal	Universal
Velocidad	Velocity

Flores
Flowers

Amapola	Poppy
Caléndula	Calendula
Diente de León	Dandelion
Gardenia	Gardenia
Girasol	Sunflower
Hibisco	Hibiscus
Jazmín	Jasmine
Lavanda	Lavender
Lila	Lilac
Lirio	Lily
Magnolia	Magnolia
Margarita	Daisy
Narciso	Daffodil
Orquídea	Orchid
Peonía	Peony
Pétalo	Petal
Ramo	Bouquet
Rosa	Rose
Trébol	Clover
Tulipán	Tulip

Formas
Shapes

Arco	Arc
Bordes	Edges
Cilindro	Cylinder
Círculo	Circle
Cono	Cone
Cuadrado	Square
Cubo	Cube
Curva	Curve
Elipse	Ellipse
Esfera	Sphere
Esquina	Corner
Hipérbola	Hyperbola
Lado	Side
Línea	Line
Oval	Oval
Pirámide	Pyramid
Polígono	Polygon
Prisma	Prism
Rectángulo	Rectangle
Triángulo	Triangle

Fruta
Fruit

Aguacate	Avocado
Albaricoque	Apricot
Baya	Berry
Cereza	Cherry
Coco	Coconut
Frambuesa	Raspberry
Guayaba	Guava
Kiwi	Kiwi
Limón	Lemon
Mango	Mango
Manzana	Apple
Melocotón	Peach
Melón	Melon
Naranja	Orange
Nectarina	Nectarine
Papaya	Papaya
Pera	Pear
Piña	Pineapple
Plátano	Banana
Uva	Grape

Fuerza y Gravedad
Force and Gravity

Centro	Center
Descubrimiento	Discovery
Dinámico	Dynamic
Distancia	Distance
Eje	Axis
Expansión	Expansion
Física	Physics
Fricción	Friction
Impacto	Impact
Magnetismo	Magnetism
Magnitud	Magnitude
Mecánica	Mechanics
Órbita	Orbit
Peso	Weight
Planetas	Planets
Presión	Pressure
Propiedades	Properties
Tiempo	Time
Universal	Universal
Velocidad	Speed

Geografía
Geography

Altitud	Altitude
Atlas	Atlas
Ciudad	City
Continente	Continent
Hemisferio	Hemisphere
Isla	Island
Latitud	Latitude
Longitud	Longitude
Mapa	Map
Mar	Sea
Meridiano	Meridian
Montaña	Mountain
Mundo	World
Norte	North
Oeste	West
País	Country
Región	Region
Río	River
Sur	South
Territorio	Territory

Geología
Geology

Ácido	Acid
Calcio	Calcium
Capa	Layer
Caverna	Cavern
Continente	Continent
Coral	Coral
Cristales	Crystals
Cuarzo	Quartz
Erosión	Erosion
Estalactita	Stalactite
Estalagmitas	Stalagmites
Fósil	Fossil
Géiser	Geyser
Lava	Lava
Meseta	Plateau
Minerales	Minerals
Piedra	Stone
Sal	Salt
Terremoto	Earthquake
Volcán	Volcano

Geometría
Geometry

Altura	Height
Ángulo	Angle
Cálculo	Calculation
Curva	Curve
Diámetro	Diameter
Dimensión	Dimension
Ecuación	Equation
Horizontal	Horizontal
Lógica	Logic
Masa	Mass
Mediana	Median
Número	Number
Paralelo	Parallel
Proporción	Proportion
Segmento	Segment
Simetría	Symmetry
Superficie	Surface
Teoría	Theory
Triángulo	Triangle
Vertical	Vertical

Gobierno
Government

Ciudadanía	Citizenship
Civil	Civil
Constitución	Constitution
Democracia	Democracy
Discurso	Speech
Discusión	Discussion
Distrito	District
Estado	State
Igualdad	Equality
Independencia	Independence
Judicial	Judicial
Justicia	Justice
Ley	Law
Libertad	Liberty
Líder	Leader
Monumento	Monument
Nacional	National
Nación	Nation
Política	Politics
Símbolo	Symbol

Granja #1
Farm #1

Abeja	Bee
Agricultura	Agriculture
Agua	Water
Arroz	Rice
Burro	Donkey
Caballo	Horse
Cabra	Goat
Campo	Field
Cuervo	Crow
Fertilizante	Fertilizer
Gato	Cat
Heno	Hay
Miel	Honey
Perro	Dog
Pollo	Chicken
Semillas	Seeds
Ternero	Calf
Tierra	Land
Vaca	Cow
Valla	Fence

Granja #2
Farm #2

Agricultor	Farmer
Animales	Animals
Cebada	Barley
Colmena	Beehive
Comida	Food
Cordero	Lamb
Fruta	Fruit
Granero	Barn
Huerto	Orchard
Leche	Milk
Llama	Llama
Maíz	Corn
Oveja	Sheep
Pastor	Shepherd
Pato	Duck
Prado	Meadow
Riego	Irrigation
Tractor	Tractor
Trigo	Wheat
Vegetal	Vegetable

Herboristería
Herbalism

Ajo	Garlic
Albahaca	Basil
Aromático	Aromatic
Azafrán	Saffron
Calidad	Quality
Culinario	Culinary
Eneldo	Dill
Estragón	Tarragon
Flor	Flower
Hinojo	Fennel
Ingrediente	Ingredient
Jardín	Garden
Lavanda	Lavender
Mejorana	Marjoram
Menta	Mint
Perejil	Parsley
Planta	Plant
Romero	Rosemary
Sabor	Flavor
Verde	Green

Ingeniería
Engineering

Ángulo	Angle
Cálculo	Calculation
Construcción	Construction
Diagrama	Diagram
Diámetro	Diameter
Diesel	Diesel
Distribución	Distribution
Eje	Axis
Energía	Energy
Estabilidad	Stability
Estructura	Structure
Fricción	Friction
Fuerza	Strength
Líquido	Liquid
Máquina	Machine
Medición	Measurement
Motor	Motor
Palancas	Levers
Profundidad	Depth
Propulsión	Propulsion

Insectos
Insects

Abeja	Bee
Avispa	Wasp
Avispón	Hornet
Áfido	Aphid
Cigarra	Cicada
Cucaracha	Cockroach
Escarabajo	Beetle
Gusano	Worm
Hormiga	Ant
Langosta	Locust
Larva	Larva
Libélula	Dragonfly
Mantis	Mantis
Mariposa	Butterfly
Mariquita	Ladybug
Mosquito	Mosquito
Polilla	Moth
Pulga	Flea
Saltamontes	Grasshopper
Termita	Termite

Instrumentos Musicales
Musical Instruments

Armónica	Harmonica
Arpa	Harp
Banjo	Banjo
Clarinete	Clarinet
Fagot	Bassoon
Flauta	Flute
Gong	Gong
Guitarra	Guitar
Mandolina	Mandolin
Marimba	Marimba
Oboe	Oboe
Pandereta	Tambourine
Percusión	Percussion
Piano	Piano
Saxofón	Saxophone
Tambor	Drum
Trombón	Trombone
Trompeta	Trumpet
Violín	Violin
Violonchelo	Cello

Jardinería
Gardening

Agua	Water
Botánico	Botanical
Clima	Climate
Comestible	Edible
Compost	Compost
Contenedor	Container
Especie	Species
Estacional	Seasonal
Exótico	Exotic
Flor	Blossom
Floral	Floral
Follaje	Foliage
Hoja	Leaf
Huerto	Orchard
Humedad	Moisture
Manguera	Hose
Ramo	Bouquet
Semillas	Seeds
Suciedad	Dirt
Suelo	Soil

Jardín
Garden

Arbusto	Bush
Árbol	Tree
Banco	Bench
Césped	Lawn
Estanque	Pond
Flor	Flower
Garaje	Garage
Hamaca	Hammock
Hierba	Grass
Huerto	Orchard
Jardín	Garden
Malezas	Weeds
Manguera	Hose
Pala	Shovel
Porche	Porch
Rastrillo	Rake
Suelo	Soil
Terraza	Terrace
Trampolín	Trampoline
Valla	Fence

Jazz
Jazz

Artista	Artist
Álbum	Album
Canción	Song
Composición	Composition
Compositor	Composer
Concierto	Concert
Estilo	Style
Énfasis	Emphasis
Famoso	Famous
Favoritos	Favorites
Género	Genre
Improvisación	Improvisation
Música	Music
Nuevo	New
Orquesta	Orchestra
Ritmo	Rhythm
Talento	Talent
Tambores	Drums
Técnica	Technique
Viejo	Old

La Empresa
The Company

Calidad	Quality
Creativo	Creative
Decisión	Decision
Empleo	Employment
Global	Global
Industria	Industry
Ingresos	Revenue
Innovador	Innovative
Inversión	Investment
Negocio	Business
Posibilidad	Possibility
Presentación	Presentation
Producto	Product
Profesional	Professional
Progreso	Progress
Recursos	Resources
Reputación	Reputation
Riesgos	Risks
Tendencias	Trends
Unidades	Units

Libros
Books

Autor	Author
Aventura	Adventure
Colección	Collection
Contexto	Context
Dualidad	Duality
Escrito	Written
Historia	Story
Histórico	Historical
Humorístico	Humorous
Inventivo	Inventive
Lector	Reader
Literario	Literary
Narrador	Narrator
Novela	Novel
Página	Page
Pertinente	Relevant
Poema	Poem
Poesía	Poetry
Serie	Series
Trágico	Tragic

Literatura
Literature

Analogía	Analogy
Análisis	Analysis
Anécdota	Anecdote
Autor	Author
Biografía	Biography
Comparación	Comparison
Conclusión	Conclusion
Descripción	Description
Diálogo	Dialogue
Estilo	Style
Ficción	Fiction
Metáfora	Metaphor
Narrador	Narrator
Novela	Novel
Poema	Poem
Poético	Poetic
Rima	Rhyme
Ritmo	Rhythm
Tema	Theme
Tragedia	Tragedy

Los Medios de Comunicación
The Media

Actitudes	Attitudes
Comercial	Commercial
Comunicación	Communication
Digital	Digital
Edición	Edition
Educación	Education
En Línea	Online
Financiación	Funding
Fotos	Photos
Hechos	Facts
Industria	Industry
Intelectual	Intellectual
Local	Local
Opinión	Opinion
Periódicos	Newspapers
Público	Public
Radio	Radio
Red	Network
Revistas	Magazines
Televisión	Television

Mamíferos
Mammals

Ballena	Whale
Burro	Donkey
Caballo	Horse
Camello	Camel
Canguro	Kangaroo
Cebra	Zebra
Conejo	Rabbit
Coyote	Coyote
Delfín	Dolphin
Elefante	Elephant
Gato	Cat
Gorila	Gorilla
Jirafa	Giraffe
Lobo	Wolf
Mono	Monkey
Oso	Bear
Oveja	Sheep
Perro	Dog
Toro	Bull
Zorro	Fox

Mascotas
Pets

Agua	Water
Cabra	Goat
Cachorro	Puppy
Cola	Tail
Collar	Collar
Comida	Food
Conejo	Rabbit
Correa	Leash
Garras	Claws
Gato	Cat
Hámster	Hamster
Lagarto	Lizard
Loro	Parrot
Patas	Paws
Perro	Dog
Pescado	Fish
Ratón	Mouse
Tortuga	Turtle
Vaca	Cow
Veterinario	Veterinarian

Matemáticas
Math

Aritmética	Arithmetic
Ángulos	Angles
Circunferencia	Circumference
Decimal	Decimal
Diámetro	Diameter
Ecuación	Equation
Esfera	Sphere
Exponente	Exponent
Fracción	Fraction
Geometría	Geometry
Paralelo	Parallel
Paralelogramo	Parallelogram
Perímetro	Perimeter
Perpendicular	Perpendicular
Polígono	Polygon
Radio	Radius
Rectángulo	Rectangle
Simetría	Symmetry
Triángulo	Triangle
Volumen	Volume

Mediciones
Measurements

Altura	Height
Ancho	Width
Byte	Byte
Centímetro	Centimeter
Decimal	Decimal
Grado	Degree
Gramo	Gram
Kilogramo	Kilogram
Kilómetro	Kilometer
Litro	Liter
Longitud	Length
Masa	Mass
Metro	Meter
Minuto	Minute
Onza	Ounce
Peso	Weight
Profundidad	Depth
Pulgada	Inch
Tonelada	Ton
Volumen	Volume

Meditación
Meditation

Aceptación	Acceptance
Atención	Attention
Bondad	Kindness
Calma	Calm
Claridad	Clarity
Compasión	Compassion
Emociones	Emotions
Gratitud	Gratitude
Mental	Mental
Mente	Mind
Movimiento	Movement
Música	Music
Naturaleza	Nature
Observación	Observation
Paz	Peace
Pensamientos	Thoughts
Perspectiva	Perspective
Postura	Posture
Respiración	Breathing
Silencio	Silence

Mitología
Mythology

Arquetipo	Archetype
Celos	Jealousy
Cielo	Heaven
Comportamiento	Behavior
Creación	Creation
Creencias	Beliefs
Criatura	Creature
Cultura	Culture
Desastre	Disaster
Fuerza	Strength
Guerrero	Warrior
Héroe	Hero
Inmortalidad	Immortality
Laberinto	Labyrinth
Leyenda	Legend
Monstruo	Monster
Mortal	Mortal
Rayo	Lightning
Trueno	Thunder
Venganza	Revenge

Moda
Fashion

Bordado	Embroidery
Botones	Buttons
Boutique	Boutique
Caro	Expensive
Elegante	Elegant
Encaje	Lace
Estilo	Style
Mediciones	Measurements
Minimalista	Minimalist
Moderno	Modern
Modesto	Modest
Original	Original
Patrón	Pattern
Práctico	Practical
Ropa	Clothing
Sencillo	Simple
Sofisticado	Sophisticated
Tejido	Fabric
Tendencia	Trend
Textura	Texture

Mueble
Furniture

Alfombra	Rug
Almohada	Pillow
Armario	Armoire
Banco	Bench
Cama	Bed
Cojines	Cushions
Colchón	Mattress
Cortinas	Curtains
Cómoda	Dresser
Edredones	Comforters
Escritorio	Desk
Espejo	Mirror
Estantería	Bookcase
Estantes	Shelves
Futón	Futon
Hamaca	Hammock
Lámpara	Lamp
Silla	Chair
Sillón	Armchair
Sofá	Couch

Música
Music

Armonía	Harmony
Armónico	Harmonic
Álbum	Album
Balada	Ballad
Cantante	Singer
Cantar	Sing
Clásico	Classical
Coro	Chorus
Grabación	Recording
Improvisar	Improvise
Instrumento	Instrument
Melodía	Melody
Micrófono	Microphone
Musical	Musical
Músico	Musician
Ópera	Opera
Poético	Poetic
Ritmo	Rhythm
Tempo	Tempo
Vocal	Vocal

Naturaleza
Nature

Abejas	Bees
Animales	Animals
Ártico	Arctic
Belleza	Beauty
Bosque	Forest
Desierto	Desert
Dinámico	Dynamic
Erosión	Erosion
Follaje	Foliage
Glaciar	Glacier
Niebla	Fog
Nubes	Clouds
Pacífico	Peaceful
Refugio	Shelter
Río	River
Salvaje	Wild
Santuario	Sanctuary
Sereno	Serene
Tropical	Tropical
Vital	Vital

Negocio
Business

Carrera	Career
Costo	Cost
Descuento	Discount
Dinero	Money
Economía	Economics
Empleado	Employee
Empleador	Employer
Empresa	Company
Fábrica	Factory
Finanzas	Finance
Impuestos	Taxes
Inversión	Investment
Mercancía	Merchandise
Moneda	Currency
Oficina	Office
Presupuesto	Budget
Tienda	Shop
Trabajo	Job
Transacción	Transaction
Venta	Sale

Nutrición
Nutrition

Amargo	Bitter
Apetito	Appetite
Calidad	Quality
Calorías	Calories
Carbohidratos	Carbohydrates
Cereales	Cereals
Comestible	Edible
Dieta	Diet
Digestión	Digestion
Equilibrado	Balanced
Fermentación	Fermentation
Nutriente	Nutrient
Peso	Weight
Proteínas	Proteins
Sabor	Flavor
Salsa	Sauce
Salud	Health
Saludable	Healthy
Toxina	Toxin
Vitamina	Vitamin

Números
Numbers

Catorce	Fourteen
Cero	Zero
Cinco	Five
Cuatro	Four
Decimal	Decimal
Diecinueve	Nineteen
Dieciocho	Eighteen
Dieciséis	Sixteen
Diecisiete	Seventeen
Diez	Ten
Doce	Twelve
Dos	Two
Nueve	Nine
Ocho	Eight
Quince	Fifteen
Seis	Six
Siete	Seven
Trece	Thirteen
Tres	Three
Veinte	Twenty

Océano
Ocean

Alga	Algae
Anguila	Eel
Arrecife	Reef
Atún	Tuna
Ballena	Whale
Barco	Boat
Camarón	Shrimp
Cangrejo	Crab
Coral	Coral
Delfín	Dolphin
Esponja	Sponge
Mareas	Tides
Medusa	Jellyfish
Ostra	Oyster
Pescado	Fish
Pulpo	Octopus
Sal	Salt
Tiburón	Shark
Tormenta	Storm
Tortuga	Turtle

Paisajes
Landscapes

Cascada	Waterfall
Cueva	Cave
Desierto	Desert
Estuario	Estuary
Gélser	Geyser
Glaciar	Glacier
Iceberg	Iceberg
Isla	Island
Lago	Lake
Laguna	Lagoon
Mar	Sea
Montaña	Mountain
Oasis	Oasis
Pantano	Swamp
Península	Peninsula
Playa	Beach
Río	River
Tundra	Tundra
Valle	Valley
Volcán	Volcano

Países #1
Countries #1

Alemania	Germany
Argentina	Argentina
Bélgica	Belgium
Brasil	Brazil
Canadá	Canada
Ecuador	Ecuador
Egipto	Egypt
España	Spain
Filipinas	Philippines
Honduras	Honduras
India	India
Italia	Italy
Libia	Libya
Malí	Mali
Marruecos	Morocco
Nicaragua	Nicaragua
Noruega	Norway
Panamá	Panama
Polonia	Poland
Venezuela	Venezuela

Países #2
Countries #2

Albania	Albania
Australia	Australia
Austria	Austria
Dinamarca	Denmark
Etiopía	Ethiopia
Francia	France
Grecia	Greece
Indonesia	Indonesia
Irlanda	Ireland
Jamaica	Jamaica
Japón	Japan
Laos	Laos
México	Mexico
Pakistán	Pakistan
Portugal	Portugal
Rusia	Russia
Siria	Syria
Sudán	Sudan
Ucrania	Ukraine
Uganda	Uganda

Pájaros
Birds

Avestruz	Ostrich
Águila	Eagle
Cigüeña	Stork
Cisne	Swan
Cuco	Cuckoo
Cuervo	Crow
Flamenco	Flamingo
Ganso	Goose
Garza	Heron
Gaviota	Gull
Gorrión	Sparrow
Halcón	Hawk
Huevo	Egg
Loro	Parrot
Paloma	Pigeon
Pato	Duck
Pelícano	Pelican
Pingüino	Penguin
Pollo	Chicken
Tucán	Toucan

Plantas
Plants

Arbusto	Bush
Árbol	Tree
Bambú	Bamboo
Baya	Berry
Bosque	Forest
Botánica	Botany
Cactus	Cactus
Fertilizante	Fertilizer
Flor	Flower
Flora	Flora
Follaje	Foliage
Frijol	Bean
Hiedra	Ivy
Hierba	Grass
Hoja	Leaf
Jardín	Garden
Musgo	Moss
Pétalo	Petal
Raíz	Root
Vegetación	Vegetation

Profesiones #1
Professions #1

Abogado	Attorney
Astrónomo	Astronomer
Atleta	Athlete
Bailarín	Dancer
Banquero	Banker
Bombero	Firefighter
Cartógrafo	Cartographer
Cazador	Hunter
Doctor	Doctor
Editor	Editor
Embajador	Ambassador
Enfermera	Nurse
Entrenador	Coach
Fontanero	Plumber
Geólogo	Geologist
Joyero	Jeweler
Músico	Musician
Pianista	Pianist
Psicólogo	Psychologist
Veterinario	Veterinarian

Profesiones #2
Professions #2

Astronauta	Astronaut
Bibliotecario	Librarian
Biólogo	Biologist
Cirujano	Surgeon
Dentista	Dentist
Detective	Detective
Filósofo	Philosopher
Fotógrafo	Photographer
Ilustrador	Illustrator
Ingeniero	Engineer
Inventor	Inventor
Investigador	Researcher
Jardinero	Gardener
Lingüista	Linguist
Médico	Physician
Periodista	Journalist
Piloto	Pilot
Pintor	Painter
Profesor	Teacher
Zoólogo	Zoologist

Psicología
Psychology

Cita	Appointment
Clínico	Clinical
Cognición	Cognition
Comportamiento	Behavior
Conflicto	Conflict
Ego	Ego
Emociones	Emotions
Evaluación	Assessment
Ideas	Ideas
Inconsciente	Unconscious
Infancia	Childhood
Pensamientos	Thoughts
Percepción	Perception
Personalidad	Personality
Problema	Problem
Realidad	Reality
Sensación	Sensation
Subconsciente	Subconscious
Sueños	Dreams
Terapia	Therapy

Química
Chemistry

Alcalino	Alkaline
Ácido	Acid
Calor	Heat
Carbono	Carbon
Catalizador	Catalyst
Cloro	Chlorine
Electrón	Electron
Enzima	Enzyme
Gas	Gas
Hidrógeno	Hydrogen
Ion	Ion
Líquido	Liquid
Metales	Metals
Molécula	Molecule
Nuclear	Nuclear
Oxígeno	Oxygen
Peso	Weight
Reacción	Reaction
Sal	Salt
Temperatura	Temperature

Restaurante #1
Restaurant #1

Alergia	Allergy
Café	Coffee
Cajero	Cashier
Camarera	Waitress
Carne	Meat
Cocina	Kitchen
Comer	To Eat
Comida	Food
Cuchillo	Knife
Ingredientes	Ingredients
Menú	Menu
Pan	Bread
Picante	Spicy
Plato	Plate
Pollo	Chicken
Postre	Dessert
Reserva	Reservation
Salsa	Sauce
Servilleta	Napkin
Tazón	Bowl

Restaurante #2
Restaurant #2

Agua	Water
Almuerzo	Lunch
Aperitivo	Appetizer
Bebida	Beverage
Camarero	Waiter
Cena	Dinner
Cuchara	Spoon
Delicioso	Delicious
Ensalada	Salad
Especias	Spices
Fruta	Fruit
Hielo	Ice
Huevos	Eggs
Pastel	Cake
Pescado	Fish
Sal	Salt
Silla	Chair
Sopa	Soup
Tenedor	Fork
Verduras	Vegetables

Ropa
Clothes

Abrigo	Coat
Blusa	Blouse
Bufanda	Scarf
Camisa	Shirt
Chaqueta	Jacket
Cinturón	Belt
Collar	Necklace
Delantal	Apron
Falda	Skirt
Guantes	Gloves
Joyas	Jewelry
Moda	Fashion
Pantalones	Pants
Pijama	Pajamas
Pulsera	Bracelet
Sandalias	Sandals
Sombrero	Hat
Suéter	Sweater
Vestido	Dress
Zapato	Shoe

Salud y Bienestar #1
Health and Wellness #1

Activo	Active
Altura	Height
Bacterias	Bacteria
Clínica	Clinic
Doctor	Doctor
Farmacia	Pharmacy
Fractura	Fracture
Hambre	Hunger
Hábito	Habit
Hormonas	Hormones
Huesos	Bones
Medicina	Medicine
Músculos	Muscles
Piel	Skin
Postura	Posture
Reflejo	Reflex
Relajación	Relaxation
Terapia	Therapy
Tratamiento	Treatment
Virus	Virus

Salud y Bienestar #2
Health and Wellness #2

Alergia	Allergy
Anatomía	Anatomy
Apetito	Appetite
Caloría	Calorie
Dieta	Diet
Digestión	Digestion
Energía	Energy
Enfermedad	Disease
Estrés	Stress
Genética	Genetics
Higiene	Hygiene
Hospital	Hospital
Infección	Infection
Masaje	Massage
Nutrición	Nutrition
Peso	Weight
Recuperación	Recovery
Saludable	Healthy
Sangre	Blood
Vitamina	Vitamin

Selva Tropical
Rainforest

Anfibios	Amphibians
Botánico	Botanical
Clima	Climate
Comunidad	Community
Diversidad	Diversity
Especie	Species
Indígena	Indigenous
Insectos	Insects
Mamíferos	Mammals
Musgo	Moss
Naturaleza	Nature
Nubes	Clouds
Pájaros	Birds
Preservación	Preservation
Refugio	Refuge
Respeto	Respect
Restauración	Restoration
Selva	Jungle
Supervivencia	Survival
Valioso	Valuable

Senderismo
Hiking

Acantilado	Cliff
Agua	Water
Animales	Animals
Botas	Boots
Camping	Camping
Cansado	Tired
Clima	Climate
Cumbre	Summit
Guías	Guides
Mapa	Map
Montaña	Mountain
Mosquitos	Mosquitoes
Naturaleza	Nature
Orientación	Orientation
Parques	Parks
Pesado	Heavy
Piedras	Stones
Preparación	Preparation
Salvaje	Wild
Sol	Sun

Suministros de Arte
Art Supplies

Aceite	Oil
Acrílico	Acrylic
Acuarelas	Watercolors
Agua	Water
Arcilla	Clay
Borrador	Eraser
Caballete	Easel
Cámara	Camera
Cepillos	Brushes
Colores	Colors
Creatividad	Creativity
Ideas	Ideas
Lápices	Pencils
Mesa	Table
Papel	Paper
Pasteles	Pastels
Pegamento	Glue
Pinturas	Paints
Silla	Chair
Tinta	Ink

Tipos de Cabello
Hair Types

Blanco	White
Brillante	Shiny
Calvo	Bald
Corto	Short
Delgada	Thin
Gris	Gray
Grueso	Thick
Largo	Long
Marrón	Brown
Negro	Black
Ondulado	Wavy
Plata	Silver
Rizado	Curly
Rizos	Curls
Rubio	Blond
Saludable	Healthy
Seco	Dry
Suave	Soft
Trenzado	Braided
Trenzas	Braids

Enhorabuena

Lo has conseguido!

Esperamos que hayas disfrutado de este libro tanto como nosotros al diseñarlo. Nos esforzamos por crear libros de la máxima calidad posible.
Esta edición está diseñada para proporcionar un aprendizaje inteligente, de calidad y divertido!

¿Te ha gustado este libro?

Una Petición Sencilla

Estos libros existen gracias a las reseñas que se publican.
¿Podrías ayudarnos dejando una reseña ahora?
Aquí tienes un breve enlace a la página de reseñas

BestBooksActivity.com/Opiniones50

¡DESAFÍO FINAL!

Reto n°1

¿Estás listo para tu juego gratis? Los utilizamos siempre, pero no son tan fáciles de encontrar. ¡Aquí están los **Sinónimos!**

Escribe 5 palabras que hayas encontrado en los rompecabezas (#21, #36, #76) y trata de encontrar 2 sinónimos para cada palabra.

Escriba 5 palabras del *Puzzle 21*

Palabras	Sinónimo 1	Sinónimo 2

Escriba 5 palabras del *Puzzle 36*

Palabras	Sinónimo 1	Sinónimo 2

Escriba 5 palabras del *Puzzle 76*

Palabras	Sinónimo 1	Sinónimo 2

Reto n°2

Ahora que te has calentado, escribe 5 palabras que hayas encontrado en los Puzzles 9, 17 y 25 e intenta encontrar 2 antónimos para cada palabra. ¿Cuántos puedes encontrar en 20 minutos?

Escriba 5 palabras del **Puzzle 9**

Palabras	Antónimo 1	Antónimo 2

Escriba 5 palabras del **Puzzle 17**

Palabras	Antónimo 1	Antónimo 2

Escriba 5 palabras del **Puzzle 25**

Palabras	Antónimo 1	Antónimo 2

Reto n°3

¡Genial! Este desafío final no es nada para ti.

¿Preparado para el reto final? Elige 10 palabras que hayas descubierto en los diferentes rompecabezas y escríbelas a continuación.

1.	6.
2.	7.
3.	8.
4.	9.
5.	10.

Ahora escribe un texto pensando en una persona, un animal o un lugar que te guste.

Puedes usar la última página de este libro como borrador.

Tu Composición:

CUADERNO DE NOTAS :

HASTA PRONTO !

Todo el Equipo

DESCUBRA JUEGOS GRATIS

GO

↓

BESTACTIVITYBOOKS.COM/FREEGAMES